BOLD BEANS

recipes to get
your pulse racing

BOLD BEANS

recipes to get
your pulse racing

Amelia Christie-Miller

KYLE BOOKS

An Hachette UK Company
www.hachette.co.uk

First published in Great Britain in 2023 by
Kyle Books, an imprint of Octopus
Publishing Group Limited
Carmelite House
50 Victoria Embankment
London EC4Y 0DZ
www.kylebooks.co.uk

ISBN: 9781804190821

Distributed in the US by Hachette Book
Group, 1290 Avenue of the Americas,
4th and 5th Floors, New York, NY 10104

Distributed in Canada by Canadian Manda
Group, 664 Annette St., Toronto, Ontario,
Canada M6S 2C8

Publishing Director: Judith Hannam
Publisher: Joanna Copestick
Editor: Tara O'Sullivan
Editorial Assistant: Emma Hanson
Art Director: Juliette Norsworthy
Photography: Joe Woodhouse
Food styling: Esther Clark
Props styling: Florence Blair
Production: Emily Noto

Printed and bound in China

10 9 8 7 6 5 4 3 2 1

CONTENTS

KEY

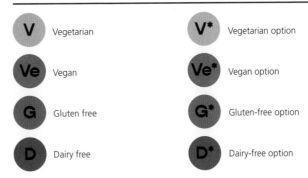

V   Vegetarian   **V***   Vegetarian option

Ve   Vegan   **Ve***   Vegan option

G   Gluten free   **G***   Gluten-free option

D   Dairy free   **D***   Dairy-free option

FOREWORD: GOOD FOOD FOR ALL – BEANS IS HOW

Beans: tiny but mighty, affordable and delicious (as this book demonstrates); charming but disruptive. Beans are the future we are hungry for.

We live in a world facing many problems: poverty, food insecurity, fragile food systems and a CO_2 level at its highest in over 2 million years. At the SDG2 Advocacy Hub, we work to achieve 'Good Food For All'. While there is no singular way to solve our complex challenges, there is a powerful ingredient: beans.

Beans are a sustainable and nutritious climate-positive solution that help tackle the global food, climate and cost of living crises while also being delicious. They are a nutrient-dense protein source that feed the soil with nitrogen, fertilising it naturally, making them a farmer's best friend. They are an affordable food group whose versatility and variety make them suitable for every meal, occasion and cuisine. With thousands of varieties, beans can grow anywhere from sea level to over 3,000 metres, in poor soil and harsh conditions. They are vital in nourishing both people and planet in a world where climate change is already happening.

While discussing these attributes with a good friend of mine, Sam Kass – who served as chef and policy advisor to President Barack Obama and First Lady Michelle Obama – we saw that we were far from realising the full potential of beans in terms of global nutrition, employment

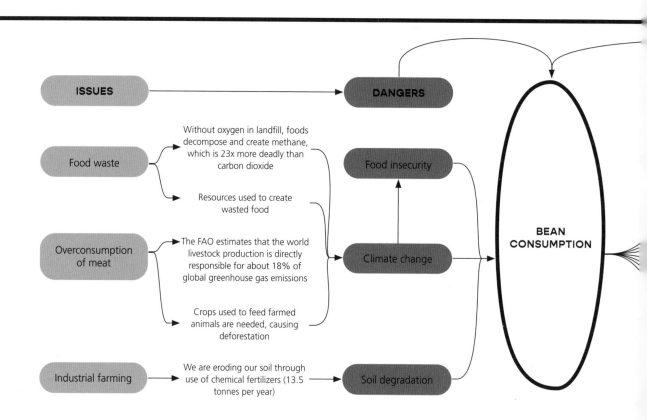

ISSUES → DANGERS

Food waste
- Without oxygen in landfill, foods decompose and create methane, which is 23x more deadly than carbon dioxide
- Resources used to create wasted food

Overconsumption of meat
- The FAO estimates that the world livestock production is directly responsible for about 18% of global greenhouse gas emissions
- Crops used to feed farmed animals are needed, causing deforestation

Industrial farming
- We are eroding our soil through use of chemical fertilizers (13.5 tonnes per year)

Food insecurity

Climate change

Soil degradation

BEAN CONSUMPTION

prospects and the future of the planet. The more we have learned about this food group, the more excited we are about the opportunities that they offer us.

'Beans is How' is a new campaign that aims to double the global consumption of beans by 2028. To achieve this bold goal, we need to change the perception of beans – making them aspirational to consumers, favourable for investors, profitable for farmers and a priority for policymakers. We also need to help more people have better knowledge about how to cook tasty beans in energy-efficient ways.

When I first came across Bold Bean Co, I was struck by the energy and excitement their team injected into

the consumption of beans. They are showing people just how elevated this humble ingredient can be, with recipes to delight, nourish and satisfy.

This book exemplifies everything our campaign stands for, and by being a *Bold Bean* cookbook holder, you too are joining the fight for a better future for people and planet.

Paul Newnham
Executive Director of SDG2 Advocacy Hub

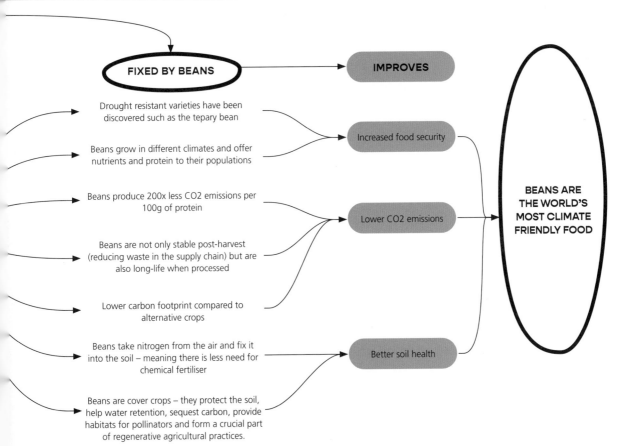

INTRODUCTION

Beans have had it tough. They've been boiled soft and hard done by; unloved and side-dished. Confined to the back of the cupboard and synonymous with tasteless hippy fodder. But a new era has come, and you've just bought the *Bold Bean* cookbook: get ready to have your opinion on beans changed forever.

I started my life hating beans. They were dusty, dull things I avoided with a vengeance. Cold, tasteless three-bean salads, sickly baked beans from a tin, and bullet-like chickpeas floating in a curry – no thank you. Fast-forward twenty years and I'm running a bean brand and about to persuade you that they're the world's best food.

So, where did this journey begin? Like most interesting stories, it began with a hangover. I was living in Madrid on a foreign exchange programme and, after another night filled with broken Spanish, I found myself hungry and lazy. I'd bought some Judión beans – specified by Nigel Slater for a recipe – and they were all I had in the house. I opened the jar and spooned one into my mouth. I distinctly remember closing my eyes to properly immerse myself in that moment; it was incredible. It was the taste of natural, creamy sumptuousness. It was the taste of a BOLDLY BRILLIANT bean. At that moment, I realised beans didn't have to be sad and soulless. A seed was planted.

My favourite childhood books were *Chocolate Island* and *The Magic Porridge Pot*, so, yes, the food obsession started young. It led me to a career in food, first as a private chef and then in the food-sustainability space, working in food tech. My latter role was working amongst the most innovative suppliers to London's top restaurants. I was surrounded not only by the leading chefs of London's food scene, but also by producers who spoke about regenerative agriculture, biodiversity and crop resilience. I became addicted to understanding more; the more you love food, the more you understand the fragile nature of our food system and want to protect it.

The rocket ship of bean obsession took off when I discovered just how crucial beans are to our food future. I learned about how our topsoils are depleting rapidly through industrial farming, and how legume crops could be the naturally fertilising saviours we need. Beans were the crop that our ancestors survived on for years when meat was harder to come by, helping civilisation get to where it is today. Rich in natural protein, they're the food group that will enable global meat reduction and help fight climate change. But mostly, as a cook and a food lover, I found them to be the ideal ingredient in taking plant-based cooking to the next level.

While the laboratories are coming up with processed, hydrolysed and emulsified solutions to sustainable diets, chefs and foodies are choosing beans. Alison Roman is selling a T-shirt with 'White Beans' on the front and The River Café is selling a jar of coco bianco beans for £18. I spent my career supplying London's top chefs and restaurants. It was here, working with those at the forefront of our food culture, where I saw beans done differently; I saw them as something delicious and aspirational, and the obsession deepened. But I also realised something else: I was very alone among my peers in this bean obsession. I started to unpick why I was so alone. It came down to two things: the quality of the beans I was eating, and the #beanspo I was seeing from the chefs I was working with.

So when COVID hit and I was made redundant from my hospitality role, I decided to turn this fire of fear, fury and excitement into something that would make beans cool. I decided to launch a brand that would make people obsessed with beans.

Quality

Rebranding this food group isn't easy, given that – for a multitude of reasons – the poor reputation of beans has been established in people's minds for centuries. In the days before factory farming, meat was a treat, a luxury reserved only for those who could afford it. The poorest in society would rely on beans as a source of protein, leaving them with a lingering association with poverty. As soon as people had made a few bucks, they'd ditch the pulses for poussin – and when the cheap chicken years came in, made possible by industrial farming, most people did exactly that. This lack of love for the bean has seeped into every part of our bean culture, from production to food writing. For over 50 years, beans have been commodified: adapted and crossbred to make the cheapest product possible. This has led to the perception of beans as the kind of tasteless, watery fodder you should leave behind at Glastonbury. But as the coffee, gin and chocolate industries have shown us, no food category should be stereotyped.

I searched high and low for the best-tasting beans I could find: sourced for quality, cooked in a way that preserves flavour, and delicious enough to eat straight from the jar. After navigating the world of brand building, we finally had a product on a shelf, and then in people's hands. I'm extremely proud of the reactions we've sparked in ex-bean-haters. They try our beans and have the same moment I had all those years ago in Madrid. A bean epiphany.

Because when beans are higher quality, their versatility in the kitchen is transformed. They're a dish in itself when served with good olive oil and lemon zest; they become the centrepiece of the salad rather than the avoided afterthought. Availability and budget can limit the quality of the beans you can get your hands on, but we want to bring down every barrier there is to a life of loving beans, so we've broken down a few 'cheat' methods for getting canned or dried closer to the incredible flavour and texture of our beans (see page 180).

Beanspo

While our product speaks volumes on behalf of all beans, there are a few other barriers to bean loving. Years of commodification have led to them rarely showing up in any recipes other than a veggie curry; it means beans are unsexy, uncool, and no one knows what to do with them. But chickpeas aren't just for hummus; white beans aren't just for a Tuscan bean stew. We need to begin seeing beans outside of this context and instead recognise them for what they really can be: the protein-rich, sumptuous and satisfying marvels that can sneak into almost any flavour combination, offering texture and heartiness – which is everything we're craving as we reduce meat and stay away from too many refined carbs.

I realised that for beans to be included more seamlessly in people's lives, we needed to inspire them to be creative. So, a year before our jarred bean range was launched, I started an Instagram account, sharing recipes that made you excited, hungry and curious about cooking with beans. That's where #beanspo came in – 'bean inspiration'. This book contains the very best of it, along with contributions from some of the people (we call them 'bean champs') that are pushing this movement forward. This book will take away the fear that comes with cooking beans. Every dish is uncompromising in its deliciousness, and after cooking from it, we challenge you not to be obsessed with beans.

Beans for everyone

So, you may be thinking, for a brand rooted in the sustainable benefits of beans, why all the CHEESE!? Well, beans are not just for vegans – they're a phenomenal, delicious food group that everyone should be embracing in their diet. There are so many endless opportunities with beans. We could have made this book entirely plant-based, but the purpose of this book is to get you excited about the potential of beans, and so ignoring their exceptional ability to soak up the flavours of a lamb shoulder (page 168) or be served in a cacio e pepe sauce (page 111) would be negligent. With this book in your kitchen, you'll be able to convert a bean-hater – and that is the first step in creating a bean-obsessive.

LIVE A LIFE FULL OF BEANS

First and foremost, we love beans because they're delicious.
But it's impossible not to delve into the numerous benefits
that these beauties have on our health. It's simple:
a life with more beans is a better one.

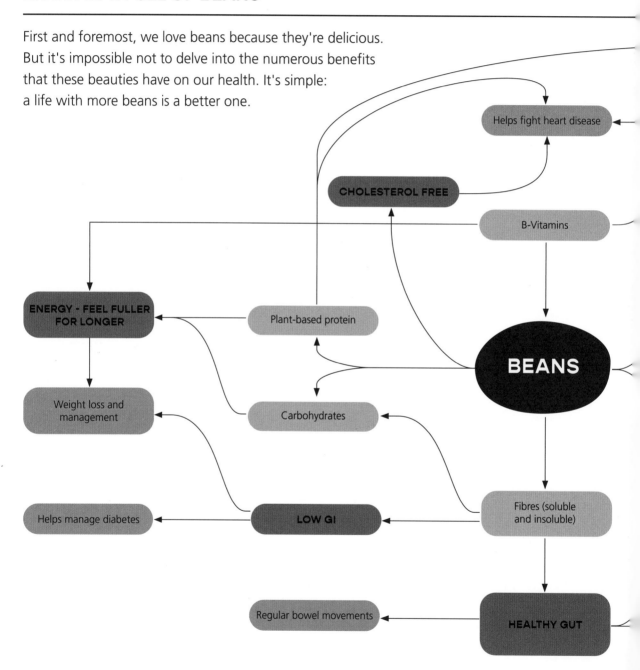

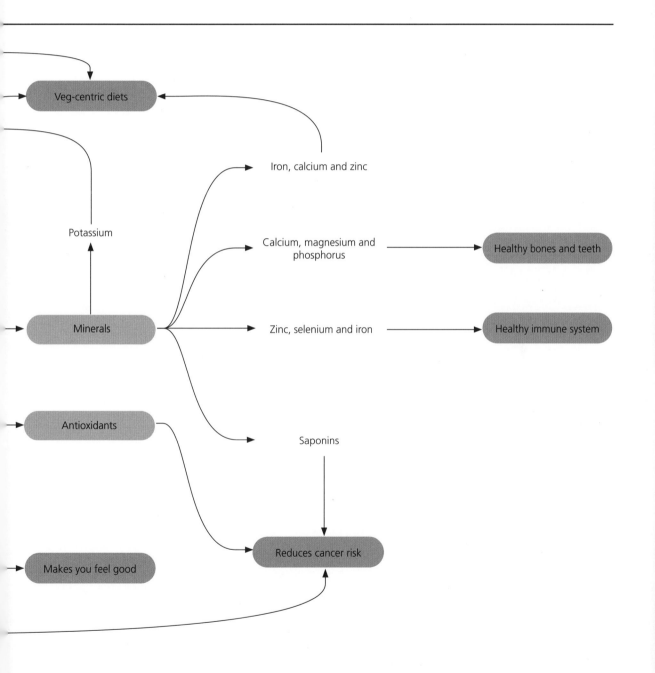

Veg-centric diets

Iron, calcium and zinc

Potassium

Calcium, magnesium and phosphorus → Healthy bones and teeth

Minerals

Zinc, selenium and iron → Healthy immune system

Antioxidants

Saponins

Reduces cancer risk

Makes you feel good

SPEEDY BEANS 1

Avo toast took the world by storm. Creaminess matched with simple seasonings and crisp toast. This one is similar, but leaves no anxiety over underripe avos, and no pain from 'avocado hand syndrome'. If you haven't tried eating cold beans before, trust us: once you've perfected your bean base, or tasted a bean from a jar, there will be no looking back. Think of it like a textured hummus. Oh, and please get a knockout olive oil for this one: it's one of the most important ingredients if you want the dish to pop.

Feeds 2
Takes 10 minutes

NOT AVOCADO TOAST

½ 700g (1lb 9oz) jar white beans, or ½ White Bean Base (page 184), drained

juice of ½ lemon or lime

2–4 slices of sourdough toast (or toast of your choice)

2 tablespoons olive oil

sea salt and freshly ground black pepper

Additional toast topper suggestions (optional)
feta, crispy maple bacon, fried halloumi, chilli flakes, basil, dill, roast cherry tomatoes

1 In a small bowl, combine the beans, lemon or lime juice and plenty of pepper. Gently mash with the back of a fork, and season to taste.

2 Top the toasted bread with the mashed bean mixture. Drizzle with olive oil and sprinkle over your desired toppings. Enjoy!

V G D*

This recipe is a slight twist on traditional Turkish eggs; here, we tumble some harissa-spiced red kidney beans over a bed of cool creamy yogurt. Warm the beans before serving for that hot-and-cold contrast. If you're a pro at poaching, by all means cook the eggs to your liking! But we've kept this a tad easier by soft-boiling them to get that jammy centre.

Feeds 2
Takes 20 minutes

TURKISH-STYLE EGGS + HARISSA BEANS

4 eggs

4 tablespoons thick Greek yogurt (or dairy-free alternative or soured cream)

juice of ½ lemon

20g (¾oz) mixed soft herbs of your choice (we like parsley and dill)

bread or pittas, to serve

For the marinated beans

1 tablespoon harissa paste (or berbere spice blend)

2 tablespoons olive oil

juice of ½ lemon

sea salt and freshly ground black pepper

1 large garlic clove, crushed

1 teaspoon smoked paprika

1 teaspoon Aleppo pepper or ½ teaspoon dried chilli flakes

½ 700g (1lb 9oz) jar red beans, or 2 × 400g (14oz) cans red kidney beans, drained and rinsed

1 Combine all the ingredients for the marinated beans in a mixing bowl, stirring well. Taste and adjust flavour as needed; add extra lemon for more acidity, harissa for heat or an extra pinch of salt. You can make this ahead and leave to marinate in the fridge for up to 3–4 days: the longer, the better.

2 When you're ready to cook, bring a saucepan of water to the boil and gently drop in the eggs, shells on. You want a jammy yolk, so soft-boil for about 5–6 minutes, depending on their size (smaller eggs will need less time). As mentioned, if you're a pro at poaching, then go ahead and poach your eggs to your liking.

3 While the eggs are cooking, mix together the yogurt and lemon juice in a bowl.

4 Once everything's almost ready, remove the red kidney beans from the fridge and give them a stir. Gently warm them through on the hob over a medium heat or in the microwave.

5 To serve, divide the yogurt between 4 plates and spread it out with the back of a spoon. Peel and halve the eggs, and arrange on top of the yogurt. Tumble over the harissa kidney beans and sprinkle over the chopped herbs. Serve, with bread for mopping up.

Tom Hunt

This originated from Bristol's Poco Tapas Bar, which started in 2004 as a festival café, touring music festivals from Glastonbury to Bestival. Full of North African warmth, it's a forgiving dish to cook for a crowd as the eggs cook perfectly within the sauce and hold well, meaning your guests can eat at their leisure. Once the base is prepared, it will keep in the fridge for up to 3 days; a winner for breakfast, lunch or dinner.

Feeds 4
Takes 20 minutes

FESTIVAL SHAKSHUKA

1 tablespoon olive oil

1 onion (red or white), sliced

2 garlic cloves, finely chopped

2 tablespoons paprika

1 teaspoon each cumin seeds, dried chilli flakes and ground coriander

400g (14oz) can chopped tomatoes

1 teaspoon white caster sugar

1 courgette (about 200g/7oz), cut into batons (or sliced green beans or long-stem broccoli)

700g (1lb 9oz) jar chickpeas with 2 tablespoons of their bean stock, or 2 × 400g (14oz) cans chickpeas, drained and rinsed

4 eggs

4 thick slices of wholemeal sourdough, toasted

sea salt and freshly ground black pepper

Optional toppings

fried halloumi, bacon, za'atar, tahini sauce, fresh coriander, dried chilli flakes

1 Heat the olive oil in a saucepan over a low–medium heat. Add the onions and cook for 10 minutes, stirring occasionally. Add the garlic, paprika, cumin seeds, chilli flakes and ground coriander, and lightly toast for 2–3 minutes.

2 Pour in the chopped tomatoes and sugar and stir to combine. Add the courgettes, followed by the chickpeas: if using jarred chickpeas, stir in 2 tablespoons bean stock; if using canned, stir in 2 tablespoons water and a good pinch of salt. Increase the heat and bring to the boil, stirring occasionally. Decrease to a simmer for a few minutes, or until the sauce thickens slightly. Taste and adjust the seasoning as needed. You will need to simmer the mixture for longer if using canned chickpeas, to allow them to soften.

3 When you're ready to eat, make a well in the mixture and crack an egg into it. Repeat with the other eggs, spacing them out evenly. Cover the pan with a lid and simmer for 6–7 minutes, or until the eggs are cooked to your liking.

4 Serve hot on a thick slice of toast with your favourite toppings. I like a combination of fried halloumi or bacon, with a sprinkle of za'atar and drizzle of tahini sauce, finished with sprigs of fresh coriander and extra chilli flakes.

Pair banging beans with a banging chilli oil, and you've got yourself an all-around banging brunch with a kick. You can buy crispy chilli oil from most Asian supermarkets, or if you know of an artisan company that includes nuts and seeds in their chilli oils, we urge you to try one, as the added texture contrasts beautifully with the soft mashed beans. If you can only find a basic chilli oil, you could improvise by adding your own toasted peanuts, cashews or crispy onions.

Feeds 2
Takes 10 minutes

BANGING BEANS

½ 700g (1lb 9oz) jar white beans or ½ White Bean Base (page 184), with 1–2 tablespoons of their bean stock

100g (3½oz) spinach

2–4 slices of sourdough toast (or toast of your choice)

2 spring onions, very finely sliced

fried or poached eggs (optional)

1–2 teaspoons crispy chilli oil (or rayu, salsa macha or peanuts in chilli oil), to taste

½ lemon or lime, cut into wedges

1 Heat the beans and 1 tablespoon of the bean stock in a saucepan over a low–medium heat. Add the spinach and gently cook through for 3–5 minutes until the spinach has wilted, stirring occasionally. Add the remaining tablespoon of bean stock if it's looking dry.

2 Plate up your toasted bread and spoon over the beans. Top with the spring onions and egg, if using, and drizzle over the chilli oil. Finish with a squeeze of lemon or lime and serve.

V*

When a dish is this simple, it's absolutely key to reach for quality. Quality beans, quality oil, quality ham. Add a seasonal green – in this case, spring-time asparagus – for colour and freshness, and you've got yourself a deliciously satisfying and simple brunch. Mop it all up with some nutty, seedy toast. If asparagus isn't in season, try some wilted spinach or long-stem broccoli.

Feeds 3–4
Takes 20 minutes

ASPARAGUS BEAN BRUNCH

400g (14oz) asparagus spears, woody ends trimmed

1–2 tablespoons olive oil, plus extra to serve

8 slices of Parma ham (optional)

4 slices of bread of your choice, toasted

1 quantity of Lemony Bean Dip (base recipe, page 66), warm

30g vegetarian hard cheese or Parmesan, shaved

thick balsamic vinegar, for drizzling (optional)

sea salt and freshly ground black pepper

1   Heat a griddle pan or non-stick frying pan over a medium–high heat. Add the asparagus drizzled with 1 tablespoon of the olive oil. Season with a pinch of salt and griddle for 4–5 minutes until nicely charred, tossing occasionally. Once the asparagus is done, transfer to a bowl and keep warm.

2   If you're using Parma ham, add this to the hot pan in batches and fry for around 2 minutes until crisp. You may need to add more oil for this. Crumble the ham over the asparagus in the bowl and set aside.

3   To serve, slather each slice of toast with generous spoonfuls of the white bean dip. Top with the asparagus (and Parma ham) mixture, followed by the shaved cheese. Drizzle with olive oil and perhaps some thick balsamic vinegar, then finish with a good crack of black pepper and serve.

The name of this recipe came before it's creation. Ed, my co-founder, is the king of puns and, in this case, he simultaneously invented a cracker of a recipe. He served it up to the team one lunch and it had to go in the cookbook. There is a smokiness and crunch from the chickpeas that texturally sings with the soft pitta, creamy mayo, ripe tomatoes and crisp lettuce.

Feeds 4
Takes 30 minutes

CHICK-PLT

700g (1lb 9oz) jar chickpeas, or 2 × 400g (14oz) cans chickpeas, drained

2 tablespoons smoked paprika

1 tablespoon onion or garlic powder

2 tablespoons maple syrup

2 tablespoons olive oil

4 pitta breads (or sliced bread for more traditional sandwiches)

3–4 tablespoons vegan mayonnaise (or standard mayo if you're not vegan)

4 large vine tomatoes, sliced

2 Little Gem lettuces, or 1 Cos lettuce

1 Preheat the oven to 220°C/200°C fan/425°F/gas mark 7.

2 Rinse the drained chickpeas to remove any sticky moisture (this will help them dry out and crisp up). Pour them into a wide baking tray and pat dry with a paper towel to remove any remaining liquid.

3 In a small bowl, combine the smoked paprika, onion or garlic powder, maple syrup and olive oil, then drizzle this mixture over the chickpeas. Roast for 25–30 minutes, or until crispy, turning halfway through.

4 Once you're ready to serve, toast your pittas for 2 minutes, then slice in half and spread the mayonnaise on both sides. Fill with the sliced tomatoes, lettuce and crispy chickpeas, and enjoy.

Move over hummus! This classic Levantine dip of walnuts, roasted red peppers, spices and pomegranate molasses is sweet, earthy and nutty; essentially, you'll want to eat it with/on everything. We've stirred it through chickpeas here, but you could also try serving it alongside the Radishing Bean + Herb Salad on page 133, in a pitta with lettuce and toms, or with our Black Bean Falafels on page 78. It will keep in the fridge for up to 5 days.

Feeds 4
Takes 20 minutes

MUHAMMARA CHICKPEAS

700g (1lb 9oz) jar chickpeas, or 2 × 400g (14oz) cans chickpeas, drained and rinsed

For the muhammara

50g (1¾oz) walnut pieces (or almonds or hazelnuts), plus extra to serve

1 slice of crusty white bread or bread of your choice, roughly chopped into chunks

3 red peppers (either from a jar for a speedy version or fresh if you're grilling yourself)

1 teaspoon smoked paprika

½ teaspoon cayenne pepper, dried chilli flakes or hot chilli powder

½ teaspoon ground cumin

1 tablespoon tomato purée

1 tablespoon pomegranate molasses

1 garlic clove, crushed

juice of ½ lemon

1–2 tablespoons olive oil, plus extra to serve

To serve

pomegranate seeds, handful of freshly chopped flat-leaf parsley or coriander, feta (optional)

1 Preheat the oven to 200°C/180°C fan/400°F/gas mark 6.

2 Tip the walnuts and bread chunks on to a baking tray and bake for 6–8 minutes until slightly golden. Keep checking on them to make sure they don't burn. This step is optional, but roasting the nuts brings out their earthy, nutty flavour.

3 If you're using jarred peppers, skip to the next step. If you're using fresh red peppers, put the red peppers on a baking tray and slide under the grill. Once they start to blacken, turn them over until they're charred on all sides. (You can also do this on a barbecue or over a gas stove: just char them straight on the flame, turning with tongs.) Once charred, place the peppers into a bowl and cover with clingfilm. Steaming them like this makes them super-easy to peel. Once they're cool enough to handle, peel and discard the charred skins from the peppers.

4 Transfer the peppers to a blender or food processor, along with the bread, walnuts, spices, tomato purée, pomegranate molasses, garlic, lemon juice and 1 tablespoon of the olive oil. Blitz until you have a smooth consistency. Add a few spoonfuls of water to loosen, if necessary.

5 Tip the chickpeas into a bowl. Add the muhammara and stir to combine, making sure the chickpeas are well coated in the sauce.

6 To serve, sprinkle over the pomegranate seeds and the fresh parsley or coriander. Add a sprinkle of feta here, if you like, and some extra toasted walnuts for crunch. Drizzle with a little more olive oil and serve. This is great alongside a fresh, crunchy salad dressed with lemon juice and olive oil.

Easy-peasy baked eggs, or Shakshuka de Paris as we like to call it. You can serve this as an indulgent breakfast. The chickpeas stop the dish from being too rich, and also make it a good option for a lunch or dinner. The braised lettuce is a great way to use up any sad, expiring salad you might have in the fridge, but you can really add any green you want.

Feeds 4
Takes 30 minutes

SPRING GREEN BAKED EGGS

700g (1lb 9oz) jar chickpeas with their bean stock, or 2 × 400g (14oz) cans chickpeas with 200ml (7fl oz) veg stock

150ml (5fl oz) double cream (or oat cream or dairy-free alternative)

40g (1½oz) butter (or 3 tablespoons extra virgin olive oil)

3 spring onions, roughly chopped

100g (3½oz) fresh or frozen peas

150g (5½oz) Little Gem lettuce (whole ones work best), cut into wedges or large pieces (or spinach, blanched broccoli or green beans)

1 small garlic clove, roughly chopped

4 eggs

grated vegetarian hard cheese or Parmesan (or Gruyère, Comté, mature Cheddar, a non-dairy alternative)

sea salt and freshly ground black pepper

Topping options
crispy bacon bits, grated Cheddar

1   Preheat the oven to 200°C/180°C fan/400°F/gas mark 6.

2   Combine the bean stock (or veg stock, if using canned beans) and cream in a saucepan or frying pan over a medium-high heat. Bring to the boil, then reduce the heat to low and simmer for about 5–10 minutes until reduced by half.

3   If using canned chickpeas, add them to the pan now, along with a pinch of salt, and simmer for 5 minutes to soften. (If using jarred, ignore this step.)

4   Melt the butter in an ovenproof frying pan over a high heat. Add the spring onions, peas and lettuce. Sauté, stirring occasionally, for 3 minutes, until the lettuce begins to wilt but still has some bite. Stir in the garlic and sauté for a minute more, then pour in the cream mixture (add the chickpeas at this point if using jarred). Season to taste.

5   Make 4 wells in the mixture and carefully crack an egg into each. Spoon some of the mixture over the egg whites to help them nestle into the dish. Sprinkle generously with cheese, then pop the pan in the oven and bake for 10–14 minutes, until the egg whites are set and the yolk is to your liking. Tuck in from the pan at the table and enjoy!

Hugh Fearnley-Whittingstall

This is a super-simple combination of great ingredients that come together beautifully. It's great as a starter, or served as a sharing plate as part of a quick pass-around supper or lunch. You can use any type of kale, but the dark green cavolo nero and the spiky-edged Russian kale are particularly tasty here. If you have any leftover roast chicken, you could tear this on top.

Feeds 2
Takes 10–15 minutes

BUTTER BEANS WITH KALE, CHILLI + MINT

1 tablespoon vegetable or olive oil

2 garlic cloves, crushed

1 hot red or green chilli, deseeded and thinly sliced

200g (7oz) kale, tough stalks removed, chopped into 2–3cm (¾–1¼in) ribbons

½ 700g (1lb 9oz) jar butter beans, or ½ Butter Bean Base (page 184), drained

1 tablespoon best-quality extra virgin olive oil

juice of 1 lemon

sea salt and freshly ground black pepper

For the crunchy mint topper

30g (1oz) toasted pumpkin seeds (or flaked almonds)

a few leaves of fresh mint, ribboned

1   Heat the oil in a large pan or wok over a fairly high heat.

2   Add the garlic and chilli and sizzle for 30 seconds or so before throwing in the kale, along with a pinch of salt.

3   Stir-fry for 3–4 minutes or so, tossing the kale from time to time or pushing it around with a spatula or wooden spoon, until the kale wilts down and becomes tender.

4   Add the butter beans and fry for another couple of minutes, stirring regularly.

5   Remove from the heat and stir in the extra virgin olive oil and a squeeze of lemon.

6   Pile on to a warmed serving dish, sprinkle over the mint and toasted pumpkin seeds, and serve.

This is a go-to for barbecues or if people are coming round. It's so simple to throw together, and the ratios can be changed according to your taste or what's on hand. As well as going with many things, these tahini-yogurt-coated chickpeas are just so satisfying.

Feeds 4
Takes 10 minutes

TAHINI YOGURT CHICKPEAS

75g (2¾oz) tahini

75g (2¾oz) yogurt of choice

2 tablespoons extra virgin olive oil, plus extra to serve

juice of 1 lemon (you may need more)

700g (1lb 9oz) jar chickpeas, or 1 Chickpea Base (page 184), drained and rinsed

½ red onion, finely diced

1–2 red or green chillies, deseeded and finely diced (adjust the quantity to your taste)

1 tablespoon sumac

30g (1oz) coriander, leaves roughly chopped, stalks finely chopped

sea salt and freshly ground black pepper

To serve
flatbreads, 4 tablespoons pomegranate or cherry molasses

1   In a mixing bowl, combine the tahini, yogurt and olive oil. Gently stir with a whisk until well combined, but don't beat too hard, as the tahini can seize up. Add a few tablespoons of cold water to loosen; you want the sauce to coat the back of a spoon. Stir in the lemon juice and a pinch of salt. Check the lemon and salt levels and adjust to your taste.

2   Add the chickpeas to the bowl, followed by the red onion, chilli, and half the sumac. Add the coriander stalks and most of the leaves, then give everything a good stir and check the seasoning.

3   Spoon into a serving bowl or platter. Garnish with the remaining coriander leaves and sumac. A drizzle of oil is also welcome. Serve with flatbreads, with the molasses alongside as a final garnish.

Claire Thomson

No cooking involved here, though you could slice some bread, drizzle with olive oil, grill it, then rub with raw garlic if you wanted to up the ante. This salad is perfect for those hot summer days; get your hands on some juicy, ripe toms to beautifully complement the creamy, fudgy beans. A go-to speedy meal or lunch-box staple that will keep beautifully in the fridge for 2–3 days.

Feeds 4
Takes 10 minutes

TOMATO + HERBY BEAN SALAD

For the dressing

1 small garlic clove, grated

1 teaspoon Dijon mustard

1 tablespoon red wine vinegar

juice of 1 lemon

3 tablespoons olive oil, plus extra to serve

For the salad

700g (1lb 9oz) jar white beans, drained and rinsed, or 1 White Bean Base (page 184)

600g (1lb 5oz) tomatoes (I like a mix of cherry and large, on the vine tomatoes)

1 large red onion or 2 banana shallots, finely chopped

small bunch of basil (about 15g/½oz), roughly chopped

small bunch of parsley (about 15g/½oz), roughly chopped

2 tablespoons capers, finely chopped

1 red or green chilli, deseeded and finely sliced (optional)

sea salt and freshly ground black pepper

Optional extras

chopped hard-boiled eggs, grilled garlic toast

1 Add all of the ingredients for the dressing to a small bowl and mix to combine

2 Add all of the salad ingredients to a large serving bowl.

3 Pour the dressing into the bowl and toss well to coat. Check for seasoning and serve, along with any optional extras.

If using less sweet, out-of-season tomatoes, add a handful of sun-dried tomatoes or a teaspoon of maple syrup to make up for this.

This was one of the most pivotal dishes in the Bold Bean Co story: it's a meal I made on one occasion using good-quality beans, and on the subsequent occasion using the cheapest that I could find. The difference was pretty catastrophic. So for this dish, like many dishes in this book, make sure you do the work in getting your bean base up to scratch, as it really pays off. The combination of sweet tomato, salty pancetta and sweet peas is a dream combination. This is a one-pan weeknight dinner that's moreish and comforting. You'll need big butter beans here, as the texture is needed to keep up with the sauce.

Feeds 2
Takes 15 minutes

MASCARPONE BRAISED BEANS

1 tablespoon olive oil

150g (5½oz) pancetta or smoked bacon, cubed

400g (14oz) can good-quality whole plum tomatoes

700g (1lb 9oz) jar Queen Butter Beans, or 1 x Butter Bean Base (page 184), drained

200g (7oz) frozen peas – ideally petits pois

125g (4½oz) mascarpone

15g (½oz) basil leaves

sea salt and freshly ground black pepper

To serve

grated Parmesan (optional), warm crusty bread, green veggies, squeeze of lemon

1 Heat the oil in a saucepan over a medium-high heat and fry the pancetta until crispy. Remove the pancetta from the pan once crispy and set aside. In the pancetta fat, add the tomatoes, breaking them down with a wooden spoon, followed by the butter beans and the peas. Bring to a simmer.

2 After a few minutes of bubbling, stir through the mascarpone (you don't want to add it too soon, or the mascarpone will split). Lastly, stir through the basil leaves, the pancetta and season to taste. Serve with gratings of Parmesan and a squeeze of lemon. We like to eat this with some warm crusty bread and a side of roasted green veggies.

**BIG BEANS
BEST**

If it's chilly outside and you've had a long day, this is what you should make. Big-flavoured mustardy mushrooms are folded through the creamiest of beans, all of it cut through with fresh wilted spinach and a squeeze of lemon. I first made this camping on the Isle of Skye with one of my best friends – wild swimming and Scottish winds were the perfect match for this quick, warming bowl of veggies. You can use crème fraîche or mascarpone interchangeably, but if using the former, go easy on the lemon.

Feeds 3
Takes 15 minutes

BEAN FLORENTINE

500g (1lb 2oz) mushrooms, sliced or roughly chopped (any variety will do)

2 tablespoons olive oil

1 onion or banana shallot, finely chopped

3 garlic cloves, sliced

700g (1lb 9oz) jar Queen Butter Beans or 1 Butter Bean Base (page 184), drained (or large chickpeas)

200g (7oz) spinach

100g (3½oz) crème fraîche (or mascarpone), plus extra to taste

1–2 teaspoons Dijon mustard

50g (1¾oz) vegetairan hard cheese or Parmesan, grated, plus extra to serve

juice of ½ lemon

large bunch of parsley (about 30g/1oz), finely chopped

sea salt and freshly ground black pepper

a hunk of bread, to serve

1 Heat a dry frying pan over a medium–high heat. Add your mushrooms in batches and dry-fry until they have browned, have lost most of their moisture and are beginning to crisp up a little. Drain and set aside, then repeat with the remaining mushrooms until they are all cooked and set aside. We love cooking mushrooms this way, as it makes them ultra-flavourful and makes their texture less squeaky.

2 Return the empty pan to a medium heat and add the olive oil. Once hot, throw in the onion, along with a pinch of salt. Cook for about 10 minutes until soft, then add the garlic, beans and cooked mushrooms. Add the spinach, and cook for 4–5 minutes until wilted, then reduce the heat to low.

3 Stir in the crème fraîche and Dijon mustard; it's key to do this at a lower temperature, to stop the mixture from splitting. If you want the dish creamier, add another tablespoon of crème fraîche at this point. Finally, add the hard cheese or Parmesan and mix well. Check for seasoning, then give it a good squeeze of lemon. Scatter over the parsley and serve with bread.

A smoky riff
For a smokier edge, add ½ ring of chorizo, chopped, and fry, then cook the onion in the chorizo oil. If you like it spicy, you can also add 1 teaspoon smoked paprika and ½ teaspoon cayenne pepper.

You've probably all tried a bean quesadilla at some point: the texture of the bean helps provide an anchoring to the cheese that is oh-so essential. This one's a little different, though, as it uses kimchi. We love serving this condiment raw, but in this recipe we find that frying it off at the beginning means it acts as a zingy seasoning to the beans. Of course, if you love the punch of it raw, simply add it to the mashed-up beans right before they go on to the tortilla. We use a mix of creamy mozzarella and sharp Cheddar here, but you can use whatever melting cheese you have to hand. These go well with a fresh, acidic salad, like the sesame cucumber one page 115.

Feeds 2
Takes 15 minutes

2 tablespoons vegetable or rapeseed oil

150g (5½oz) kimchi, finely chopped (if you're veggie, check the label and try to find a shrimp-free version)

½ 700g (1lb 9oz) jar black beans, or 400g (14oz) can black beans

½–1 teaspoon chilli powder

2 large tortillas

30g (1oz) mature Cheddar, torn or grated

50g (1¾oz) mozzarella

sea salt and freshly ground black pepper

To serve (optional)
small bunch of finely chopped coriander, lime wedges

KIMCHI + BLACK BEAN QUESADILLAS

1 Heat 1 tablespoon of the oil in a heavy-based frying pan over a medium heat. Add the kimchi and stir for 3–4 minutes until some of it starts to catch at the bottom. At this point, add the black beans, along with 1 tablespoon of their bean stock or water if the mixture is too dry. Add the chilli powder and stir to combine, then mash the mixture with a potato masher or the back of a fork. Season to taste; if using canned beans, you may need to add more salt.

2 Build the quesadillas. Take one of the tortillas and add half of the black bean and kimchi mash to it, keeping it on one side of the tortilla. Sprinkle over the Cheddar and tear over the mozzarella, then fold the other half of the tortilla on top.

3 Add the remaining oil to the frying pan and cook the quesadilla for 2–3 minutes on each side until browned. Repeat with the remaining tortilla.

4 Serve garnished with the chopped coriander and a good squeeze of lime juice, if you like.

Sweet peas, fresh mint and tangy feta, scooped up with crispy beans and a kick of chilli. Crispy beans, you say? We often call our Queen Butter Beans 'nature's gnocchi', because these big butter beans can act in a very similar way. Crunch up their skins while keeping their centres pillowy soft, serve with fresh sauces, and you've got a dish in minutes.

Feeds 2
Takes 15 minutes

PEA, MINT + FETA SMASH

For the smash

300g (10½oz) cooked peas (defrosted and microwaved for 2 minutes, or blanched)

1 small garlic clove, grated

10 mint sprigs, leaves picked

2 tablespoons olive oil, plus extra if needed

juice of 1 lemon, plus wedges to serve

For the beans

2 tablespoons olive oil

½ 700g (1lb 9oz) jar butter beans, or half a Butter Bean Base (page 184), drained

1 teaspoon dried chilli flakes

100g (3½oz) feta, crumbled into chunks (or 225g/8oz grilled sliced halloumi)

sea salt and freshly ground black pepper

1 teaspoon sumac or za'atar (optional)

toast, to serve (we like sourdough)

1 Combine the peas, garlic, mint, olive oil and lemon juice in a food processor and pulse until you have a thick purée (it's good if it's a little chunky!). Season to taste and add more olive oil to loosen, if necessary. You could also do this in a pestle and mortar for an even chunkier texture.

2 Heat 1 tablespoon of the olive oil in a frying pan over a high heat. Add half the butter beans and cook for 4–5 minutes, stirring occasionally, until golden and crispy. Transfer to a plate, then repeat with the remaining oil and beans to cook the second batch. When they are all done, turn off the heat, return the first batch to the pan, scatter over the chilli flakes and set aside.

3 Spread the purée onto your serving plate. Tumble over the crispy beans, then sprinkle over the feta and some cracked black pepper. Serve immediately on toast with lemon wedges for squeezing and sprinkle over the sumac or za'atar for a bit of colour.

Top left: Green Tahini Beans
Top right: Easy Pea-sy Pesto Chickpeas
Bottom: Pea, Mint + Feta Smash

Nothing beats the taste of fresh, homemade pesto – red, walnut or wild garlic will all work here. But if time isn't on your side, feel free to speed up this recipe with some shop-bought pesto instead. We love jazzing up a classic by throwing in some petits pois, as their natural sweetness will balance the punchy pesto.

Feeds 3–4
Takes 15 minutes

EASY PEA-SY PESTO CHICKPEAS

700g (1lb 9oz) jar Queen Chickpeas, or 1 Chickpea Base (page 184), with their bean stock (or any mild-flavoured white bean)

50g (1¾oz) frozen petits pois or peas, defrosted

2 large handfuls of spinach

sea salt and freshly ground black pepper

For the pesto

large bunch of basil (about 70–80g/2½oz)

70g (2½oz) pine nuts, toasted, plus extra to serve

2 garlic cloves

25g (1oz) vegetarian hard cheese or Parmesan, grated

juice of 1 lemon, plus extra if needed

3–4 tablespoons olive oil

To serve (optional)

toast, extra lemon wedges, grilled green beans or long-stem broccoli, fresh or roasted cherry tomatoes, toasted sunflower or pumpkin seeds

1 To make the pesto, combine the basil, pine nuts, garlic, cheese and lemon juice in a blender. Add 3 tablespoons of the oil and blitz until smooth. If it's looking a little too thick, add more olive oil until you reach your desired consistency.

2 Tip the chickpeas or beans into a saucepan over a medium heat, along with a few tablespoons of their bean stock. Add the pesto and gently warm through for a couple of minutes, then stir in the peas and spinach.

3 Continue to gently warm through for a few minutes until the spinach has wilted and the pesto is mixed throughout. Season with salt, pepper and lemon to taste, then serve topped with toasted pine nuts (or toasted seeds, if using). This is great on toast, or served alongside some grilled greens and roasted tomatoes with extra lemon wedges. Pictured on page 41.

Herbaceous, tangy tahini coats slightly crisp broccoli and butter beans for this easy midweek meal. It's bright and richat the same time. If you want to mix it up, use the silky sauce and bean combo with roasted aubergine instead of a hearty green.

Feeds 3–4
Takes 25 minutes

GREEN TAHINI BEANS

700g (1lb 9oz) jar white beans, or 1 White Bean Base (page 184), drained

For the charred broccoli
1 head of broccoli, chopped into medium-sized florets (or kale, Brussels sprouts or 2 roasted aubergines)

2 tablespoons olive oil

1 tablespoon cumin seeds

sea salt and freshly ground black pepper

For the tahini dressing
large bunch of parsley (about 30g/1oz)

large bunch of coriander (about 30g/1oz)

150g (5½oz) tahini

juice of 1 large lemon

1 tablespoon olive oil

To serve
chunky slices of toast, pitta chips or crispbreads, pomegranate seeds or chilli oil

1 Preheat the oven to 200°C/180°C fan/400°F/gas mark 6.

2 Spread out the broccoli florets on a baking tray. Drizzle with the olive oil, then scatter over the cumin seeds and season with salt and pepper. Toss to coat, then roast for 20–25 minutes until cooked through and charred.

3 Meanwhile, combine all of the dressing ingredients in a blender and blitz until smooth. Add 2–3 tablespoons water to loosen if necessary.

4 To serve cold, place the drained beans on a serving plate, then add the tahini dressing and stir it through. To serve warm, gently warm the beans and dressing in a saucepan for a couple of minutes, then tip on to a serving plate.

5 Top the beans with the charred broccoli. Serve with pitta chips or crispbreads for scooping, or spoon the beans on to a chunky slab of toast. Finish with pomegranate seeds for something fresh or chilli oil for something smoky. Pictured on page 41.

Feeds 2
Takes 15 minutes

1 tablespoon olive oil, plus extra (optional) to serve

1 small onion or banana shallot, diced

700g (1lb 9oz) jar butter beans, or 1 Butter Bean Base (page 184), with their bean stock

crème fraîche, to taste (optional)

crusty bread, to serve

For the salsa verde

3 small bunches of soft herbs (about 15g/½oz each) – parsley, mint and basil are best – finely chopped

2–3 teaspoons capers (drained), finely chopped

2 teaspoons Dijon mustard

2 anchovy fillets, finely chopped (optional)

1–2 tablespoons sherry vinegar or red wine vinegar

1 garlic clove, grated

zest of 1 lemon

6 tablespoons extra virgin olive oil

For the charred tomatoes (optional)

1 teaspoon olive oil

250g (9oz) cherry tomatoes, ideally on the vine

4 garlic cloves, thinly sliced

sea salt

Creamy white beans and zingy salsa verde are a beautiful combination (which is why we couldn't resist suggesting it as a pairing for the Lemony Bean Dip on page 66). Our friend Anna Humphries adds crème fraîche and wilted spinach, and serves it with white fish. I also served it with slow-cooked pork belly at my wedding. Here we have a version with charred cherry tomatoes. It's a banger served alone with some toast or griddled halloumi, or you could make a bean-feast of it by serving it with a whole roast chicken.

CREAMY BEANS WITH SALSA VERDE

1 Heat the olive oil in a frying pan over a low heat. Add the onion and sweat for 8–10 minutes until softened.

2 Add the beans, along with their bean stock, breaking up a few of them with your hands as you pour them in (this will help thicken the mixture). You may want to add a few tablespoons of water or crème fraîche to loosen it here.

3 To make the salsa verde, combine all the ingredients in a bowl and mix to a coarse salsa. Don't be tempted to do this in a food processor; you want to keep that rustic texture, not end up a refined, smooth paste.

4 Finally, make the charred cherry tomatoes, if using. Heat the olive oil in a large frying pan over a high heat. Once hot, add the whole tomatoes to the pan and cook for about 5 minutes, shaking the pan occasionally so that the tomatoes get some good charring on all sides.

5 Add the garlic slices and cook for 1 minute more until the garlic turns golden brown – but don't let it burn. Sprinkle over a good pinch of sea salt.

6 To serve, spoon the beans into bowls, then top with the charred toms and salsa verde. Add an extra drizzle of olive oil if you're feelin' saucy. Mop up the juices with some crusty bread.

For something a little more sophisticated, add a glug of white wine to the onions and reduce until the alcohol has burned off.

We love mixing Asian flavours with black beans as they can stand up to the punch of soy and ginger. This is a super-speedy weeknight meal that you can whip up alongside a fried egg or some rice. Sweet soy sauce can be hard to find sometimes, but you can easily make something similar yourself using soy and honey as described below. We like serving the green beans whole, as they look beautiful, but feel free to chop them up into bite-sized pieces for ease.

Feeds 2 as a light dinner or side
Takes 20 minutes

SOY + GINGER BLACK BEANS

2 teaspoons neutral oil, such as sunflower, vegetable or light rapeseed oil

½ thumb-sized piece of fresh ginger, grated

2 garlic cloves, crushed

½ 700g (1lb 9oz) jar black beans with 3 tablespoons of their bean stock, or 400g (14oz) can black beans, drained

2 tablespoons sweet soy sauce (kecap manis), plus extra to taste (or 1½ tablespoons soy sauce mixed with ½ tablespoon maple syrup)

1 red or green chilli, halved lengthways

150g (5½oz) fine green beans, trimmed (or ½ hispi/pointed cabbage or spring greens)

1 tablespoon sesame oil

2 teaspoons toasted sesame seeds

20g (¾oz) plant-based butter or butter of choice

rice vinegar (or juice of ½ lime) (optional), to taste

30g (1oz) salted peanuts or cashews, chopped

To serve (optional)
cooked white rice, fried eggs, sliced spring onions

1 Heat the oil in a heavy-based frying pan over a low–medium heat. Add the ginger and garlic and fry for 30 seconds, then add the black beans with their bean stock (or 3 tablespoons water if using canned), along with the kecap manis and chilli. Stir to combine, then cover and simmer for 8–10 minutes to infuse the beans with the flavourings. If you're using canned beans, give them a little longer, and taste for seasoning; you may need another 1 tablespoon kecap manis if the beans are unsalted. Keep warm.

2 Meanwhile, boil the green beans in a saucepan of salted, boiling water for 3–5 minutes until tender but still retaining a bit of crunch. Once done, remove from the heat and dress with the sesame oil and toasted sesame seeds.

3 Come back to the black beans. Increase the heat to medium–high and cook for a further 2–3 minutes, stirring often. Finish by melting in the butter. The beans should look glossy and a little sticky. Remove from the heat and add the rice vinegar or lime juice to taste (start with 1 teaspoon).

4 If serving with rice, plate up the rice first, then ladle on the black beans and top with the sesame green beans (and eggs, if using). Sprinkle over the peanuts or cashews for crunch, along with the spring onions if using, then serve.

The nostalgic British classic: coronation chicken. We like getting chickpeas involved for something a bit speedier but just as delicious and filling; it also just happens to be plant-based. Texture is key in this dish, so we love the addition of the Bombay mix for crunch; it contrasts beautifully with the soft white bread. If you're not in the sandwich mood, serve the chickpeas on a platter, loaded on to the iceberg leaves and topped with the crunchy bits.

Feeds 4
Takes 10 minutes

CORONATION CHICKPEA SANDWICH

5 tablespoons mayonnaise (use vegan mayo to make this vegan)

2–3 teaspoons mild curry powder, to taste

1 teaspoon ground turmeric

½ teaspoon ground cinnamon

2 tablespoons mango chutney

2 tablespoons sultanas or raisins

large handful of roughly chopped coriander (about 15g/½oz)

700g (1lb 9oz) jar chickpeas or 1 Chickpea Base (page 184), bean stock reserved

8 slices of fresh soft white bread, or 4 focaccias, halved

½ head of crunchy iceberg lettuce, torn into sandwich-sized leaves

sea salt and freshly ground black pepper

For the crunchy bits (optional)

2 tablespoons Bombay mix, roughly chopped

1 tablespoon flaked almonds, toasted

1   In a bowl, mix together the mayonnaise, curry powder, turmeric, cinnamon, chutney and sultanas or raisins. Stir through the coriander, and season with salt and black pepper to taste.

2   Add the chickpeas to the sauce and stir to coat. Stir in 2 tablespoons bean stock to loosen if needed, then season to taste.

3   Divide the coronation chickpea filling between 4 of the slices of bread or the bottom halves of the focaccia. Top with the crunchy bits (if using) and lettuce leaves, then top each one with another slice of bread or the tops of the focaccia. Cut into halves and serve.

For a tangier option, replace the mayonnaise with 2 tablespoons Greek yogurt mixed with 3 tablespoons mayonnaise.

Purists will be tearing their hair out, but we wanted to put our own spin on the much loved classic Italian pasta with tomato, anchovies, chilli and capers. The creaminess of butter beans here creates the ultimate satisfaction without the added sluggishness you can often feel after a weighty bowl of pasta – and if you're using jarred beans, you don't even need to cook them beforehand. This is a weeknight staple, whipped up in 10 minutes, and can travel easily into work with you the next day for a delicious lunch that will really hit the spot.

Feeds 2
Takes 20 minutes

BEAN PUTTANESCA

2–3 tablespoons olive oil, plus extra to serve

6 anchovy fillets (or 100g/3½oz smoked streaky bacon or 60g (2¼oz) diced pancetta. If using pork, make sure to fry it off until beginning to crisp before adding your onion)

1 large red onion, finely sliced

2 garlic cloves, finely sliced

50g (1¾oz) capers

1 red chilli, deseeded, or 1 teaspoon dried chilli flakes

70g (2½oz) pitted Kalamata olives, half left whole, half chopped in half

400g (14oz) can chopped tomatoes

½ teaspoon white caster sugar or honey (to balance the acidity)

700g (1lb 9oz) jar Queen Butter Beans, or 1 Butter Bean Base (page 184), with their bean stock (or chickpeas; just make sure they're the big fat ones)

large bunch of flat-leaf parsley (about 30g/1oz), chopped

1 Heat 2 tablespoons of the olive oil in a frying pan over a medium–high heat. Add the anchovy fillets, whole, and let them cook off and reduce for about 2 minutes. Once they have cooked down and shrunk slightly, add the onion. You may need to add another tablespoon of olive oil at this point to ensure the onion gets well coated. Continue to stir until the onion has caramelised and is becoming translucent. Add the garlic, capers, chilli and olives and continue to stir for 2 minutes.

2 Next, add the can of chopped tomatoes and the sugar or honey. Stir and simmer, still over a medium–high heat, for 3–5 minutes. Next, add the beans to the pan, along with their bean stock. Continue to simmer for another 5 minutes until the sauce thickens.

3 Serve with chopped parsley and a generous glug of olive oil.

Colu Henry

When 'nduja is involved, you know the recipe is going to be incredible. The stock used in this dish is integral to making its soupiness do its thing, so whether you're using bean stock or good-quality chicken or vegetable stock, make sure it's top notch.

Feeds 4
Takes 10 minutes

SOUPY 'NDUJA BEANS

1 tablespoon olive oil, plus extra for drizzling

120g (4¼oz) 'nduja (or sobrasada with 1 teaspoon of chilli flakes, or cooking chorizo, broken up into small pieces)

1½ 700g (1lb 9oz) jars Queen Butter Beans, or 1½ × White Bean Base (page 184), with their bean stock

200–300ml (7–10fl oz) veggie or chicken stock – fresh is best here

2 heads (about 280g/10oz) Castelfranco radicchio (or other readily available variety), leaves separated and torn (or chicory if you want something less bitter)

small bunch of basil (about 15g/½oz), torn

small bunch of flat-leaf parsley (about 15g/½oz), torn

To serve (optional)
grated Pecorino or Parmesan, toasted panko breadcrumbs

1 Heat the oil in a large, heavy-based frying pan over a medium heat. Add the 'nduja and cook for about 4 minutes until it begins to melt. Add the beans with their bean stock, along with the veg or chicken stock, and stir until the beans are coated with 'nduja oil. Allow to simmer for a minute or so, adding a splash of water if the beans look dry.

2 Add the radicchio leaves and toss until they are gently wilted.

3 Ladle the soupy beans into soup bowls and top with the torn herbs. Drizzle with additional olive oil, then scatter over some grated cheese and toasted panko breadcrumbs to serve, if you like.

This sauce is a revelation. Rich and complex, but a doddle to whip up. Slathered on to big, creamy butter beans, it becomes a sensational main dish that can be passed around the table to share with friends. You can fry off a few rashers of bacon at the beginning of the recipe if you want to take the richness up a notch, but you really don't need to. This is one of the recipes where we need you to find big butter bean varieties (see Queen Butter Beans, page 183) as it makes a load of a difference. Serve with a side salad and garlic bread.

Feeds 2
Takes 10–15 minutes

2 tablespoons olive oil

1 banana shallot, very finely diced, or ½ white onion

2 fat garlic cloves, crushed

¼–½ teaspoon dried chilli flakes

100g (3½oz) tomato purée

5 tablespoons vodka

100ml (3½fl oz) double cream

700g (1lb 9oz) jar Queen Butter Beans, or 1 Butter Bean Base (page 184), with their bean stock, or the biggest white bean you can find

30g (1oz) grated vegetarian hard cheese or Parmesan (or Pecorino or Grana Padano), plus extra to serve

sea salt

To serve
basil leaves, breadcrumbs (optional, for a bit of crunch)

BEANS ALLA VODKA

1 Heat the oil in a deep frying pan over a low heat. Add the shallot and a pinch of salt, and fry gently for 10–12 minutes or until softened and translucent. Add the garlic and chilli, and cook for 1 minute, then tip in the tomato purée and increase the heat to medium-high Fry for 2 minutes, then pour in the vodka. Bring it to simmer and cook for 4 minutes until reduced by half. Quickly stir through the cream.

2 Tip the beans, including their bean stock, into the pan, followed by the cheese and a good pinch of salt. Stir it all together, adding a splash of water if it feels a little too thick, and bring to a simmer once more. Serve topped with extra cheese and a handful of basil, plus some breadcrumbs, if you like.

V G

This is one for the kids (or your inner kid!): melted cheese, tomato base, loaded with whatever toppings are to your liking. The Smitten Kitchen created this stunner and credited it for winning her son over on the beans; we've simplified it a bit to keep it rapid and weeknight friendly. This is a VERY rough concept that we want you to roll out, remix and do your own way. The key things? White beans, tomato and cheese. That's all, folks. Wolf this down with garlic bread and a zingy green salad.

Feeds 2–4 kids or 2 grown-ups
Takes 20 minutes

PIZZA BEANS

1 tablespoon olive oil

1 onion (red or white), finely chopped

½ 700g (1lb 9oz) jar white beans, or 400g (14oz) can white beans, drained

350g (12oz) shop-bought tomato and basil or tomato and garlic pasta sauce (or 350g/12oz passata, plus a small bunch of fresh basil and 1 garlic clove, crushed)

½ tablespoon dried oregano (optional)

200g (7oz) fresh spinach

150g (5½oz) mozzarella, torn

30g (1oz) vegetarian hard cheese or Parmesan, grated

sea salt

Topping ideas

kid friendly: sweetcorn, peppers, mushrooms

jazz it up: black olives, pepperoni, ham, artichokes, dried chilli flakes

1 Heat the olive oil in a frying pan over a medium–high heat. Add the onion, along with a pinch of salt, and sweat for 5 minutes until soft.

2 If you're using jarred beans, skip to the next step. If you're using canned beans, add these to the pan now, along with a few tablespoons of water and ½ teaspoon salt (if the beans are unsalted). Let the beans bubble away for 10–15 minutes, letting the water evaporate and adding more as needed, until your beans have softened slightly.

3 If you're using jarred beans, add them to the pan now, along with the tomato sauce. Add the oregano, if using, and simmer a little. If the mixture looks too dry or thick, you could add some water to loosen. Simmer for 5 minutes until bubbling and hot, then add the spinach and allow to wilt. Preheat your grill to high at this point.

4 Transfer the bean mixture to a medium-sized ovenproof dish, and sprinkle first with the mozzarella, then with the hard cheese or Parmesan. Scatter over any other toppings you want to add.

5 Grill for 5 minutes or so until golden brown, then serve. This is great with a fresh green salad and garlic bread.

BEAN SNACKS + SHARE PLATES 2

SILKY HUMMUS – LOADED 3 WAYS

Too often, hummus is reserved for snacks and picnics. In Israel, they centre a meal around it, with cafés serving up bowls of hummus alongside sides that offer freshness, crunch and acidity in the form of falafels, grilled veggies, cucumber salads and pickles. Pittas always feature too. After eating a hummus meal, you feel light and satisfied in equal measure. We encourage you to give it a go.

People frequently tell us how much better our Queen Chickpeas are in hummus compared to the bog standard canned variety. Obviously lots of this comes down to the flavour and quality of the beans, but of equal importance in the pursuit of hummus perfection is texture. Our Queen Chickpeas are very large chickpeas with very thin skins; this means the ratio of skin to soft centre is a lot lower than that of standard chickpeas, which tend to have thicker skins. While using our jars of Queen Chickpeas makes hummus better, we wanted to give you a recipe for PERFECTION: aka the silkiest, dreamiest hummus you can make. The new ingredient?

Time. Letting chickpeas of any size bubble away in some bicarb means that all the flavour in the skins is retained but they melt into the broth, making the resulting hummus as smooth as can be. We have one of our bean champs, George, to thank for this. He worked hard at refining and tweaking the recipe to achieve the ultimate silkiness, and now we have it here for you to enjoy.

A cheat's version
Keep your beans in the fridge so
they're super-cold. Pop in a blender with
the lemon juice, ½ finely chopped garlic
clove, 3 tablespoons of tahini
and 2 tablespoons olive oil, and
blitz until smooth.

Feeds 6 as a side
Takes 2 hours, including cooling time

THE SILKY HUMMUS

700g (1lb 9oz) jar Queen Chickpeas
with their bean stock, or 2 × 400g
(14oz) cans chickpeas

¼ teaspoon bicarbonate of soda (if
using jarred chickpeas)

juice of ½ lemon

1 garlic clove, very finely chopped

4 ice cubes

3 tablespoons tahini

2 tablespoons olive oil, plus extra to
serve (you want the best-quality oil
you can get here)

flaky sea salt

1 teaspoon ground cumin or paprika,
to serve (optional)

1 If using jarred beans: In a saucepan over a low heat, combine the
chickpeas, their bean stock and the bicarb of soda. Fill the jar with water
and add that, too. Simmer, covered, for 30–40 minutes until the skins
have dissolved. Leave to cool in the liquid. Be patient; it's worth it. You
could do this the night before if you like.

2 If using canned beans: In a saucepan over a low heat, combine the
chickpeas with 900ml (1½ pints) water and 1 teaspoon salt. Cook for 50
minutes until the skins have dissolved, then leave to cool in the liquid.
Again, you could do this the night before.

3 Mix together the lemon juice and garlic in a small bowl; this mellows
the garlic.

4 Once the chickpeas have cooled, fish them out (reserving any cooking
liquor and around 10 whole chickpeas for decoration) and add to a food
processor. Keeping the food processor cool here is essential, otherwise
the oil can become bitter, so once again, make sure you're patient. Add
an ice cube, along with 50ml (2fl oz) of the cooking liquor, and blitz for 1
minute. Then add the garlicky lemon juice, tahini, olive oil and 2 pinches
of flaky sea salt. Keep throwing in the ice cubes as you process this – not
only does it help keep things cool, but it makes the hummus creamier by
solidifying the oils from the olive oil and tahini.

5 Once you're happy with the texture, spoon the hummus on to your serving
plate. Top with the reserved chickpeas and drizzle with some more olive oil.
Scatter over some cumin or paprika too, if you like, and serve.

Feeds 4 as a side, 2 as a main
Takes 10 minutes

1 CRISPY 'NDUJA CHICKPEAS

1 tablespoon olive oil

1 quantity of Silky Hummus (page 59), with a handful of whole chickpeas reserved

125g (4½oz) 'nduja

fresh cucumber salad, to serve

1 Heat the oil in a large frying pan. Add the reserved chickpeas and cook, stirring, until the chickpeas have become crispy and are starting to caramelise. Then add the 'nduja which should melt into the pan and release its oils as you stir it around. After it has melted and parts of it are becoming crispy, leave to cool before loading on to your hummus and serving.

Fresh Cucumber Salad

Slice 1 cucumber on the diagonal. Mix with a large bunch of chopped herbs (we like mint and coriander) and the juice of 1 lemon. Season to taste.

Feeds 2
Takes 30 minutes

2 ROASTED BRUSSELS SPROUTS + ZHOUG

200g (7oz) Brussels sprouts, trimmed and halved

1–2 tablespoons olive oil

1 quantity of Silky Hummus (page 59), with a handful of whole chickpeas reserved

sea salt and freshly ground black pepper

For the zhoug

large bunch of coriander (30g/1oz), leaves only

2 jalapeños, or 8–10 pickled jalapeños, halved and deseeded

1–2 garlic cloves, peeled

½ teaspoon sea salt

½ teaspoon ground cardamom or the seeds from 4 cardamom pods (optional)

½ teaspoon ground cumin

½ teaspoon dried chilli flakes

1 tablespoon olive oil

1 Preheat the oven to 200°C/180°C fan/400°F/gas mark 6.

2 Tumble the sprouts into a baking tray and toss with the olive oil and a big pinch of salt. Roast for 15–20 minutes until cooked to your liking.

3 Meanwhile, make the zhoug. Add all the ingredients to a food processor and blitz until well combined. Season to taste.

4 Dollop the hummus on to a serving plate or bowl. When the sprouts are ready, pile them up on top of the hummus, top with the reserved chickpeas, then drizzle over the zhoug and serve.

Feeds 2
Takes 1 hour

 ROASTED AUBERGINE, SUMAC ONIONS + OLIVES

1 large aubergine

1 tablespoon olive oil

1 quantity of Silky Hummus (page 59), with a handful of whole chickpeas reserved

sea salt

For the sumac onions

1 large red onion, finely sliced

15g (½oz) parsley or coriander, finely chopped, plus extra to garnish

4 tablespoons red wine vinegar or sherry vinegar

2 tablespoons olive oil

4 teaspoons sumac

½ teaspoon sea salt

½ teaspoon white caster sugar

To serve

small handful of pitted olives of your choice, halved, a pinch of dried chilli flakes, pomegranate seeds (optional)

1 Preheat the oven to 200°C/180°C fan/400°F/gas mark 6. In a bowl, mix together the ingredients for the sumac onions. Set aside for a quick pickling.

2 Meanwhile, roast the aubergine. Pierce the aubergine a few times with the tip of a knife, then brush with the olive oil, season well with salt and put on a baking sheet. Roast for about 40–45 minutes, or until the aubergine is completely tender. The skin should appear slightly blistered.

3 To assemble, spread out your hummus on a serving plate or bowl. Top with the aubergine and slice it in half, opening it up a bit like a baked potato and spreading out its flesh a little. Garnish with some of the sumac onions (use the rest for tacos, sandwiches and salads; they will keep in the fridge for around a week), along with the reserved chickpeas, the olives, some extra herbs, the chilli flakes and pomegranate seeds, if using. Serve.

Henry Dimbleby and Jane Baxter

We love these fritters with their burst of orange zest. They make us think of sitting by a swimming pool in the sunshine, sangria in hand.

Makes 20
Takes 50 minutes

CHICKPEA FRITTERS WITH ROMESCO

1 teaspoon cumin seeds

700g (1lb 9oz) jar chickpeas, or 2 × 400g (14oz) cans chickpeas, drained

zest and juice of 2 oranges

1 roasted red pepper from a jar, finely sliced

3 spring onions, finely chopped

large bunch of parsley (about 30g/1oz), leaves chopped

100g (3½oz) gram (for gluten-free), or plain flour

2 teaspoons baking powder

½ teaspoon salt

neutral cooking oil, for frying

For the romesco
100g (3½oz) blanched almonds

1–2 small garlic cloves

50ml (2fl oz) extra virgin olive oil

1 tablespoon sherry vinegar

200g (7oz) roasted red peppers

1 teaspoon maple syrup (optional)

1 First, make the fritter batter. Toast the cumin seeds in a dry frying pan over a medium heat for 30 seconds–1 minute until fragrant, then tip on to a plate and allow to cool.

2 Roughly mash the chickpeas with a potato masher, leaving some of them whole. Add the toasted seeds, along with all the remaining fritter ingredients, other than the orange juice and oil. Mix until well combined. If using canned chickpeas, add a good pinch of salt here. Lastly, add the orange juice, a little at a time, stirring between each addition, to loosen the mixture. You may not need all of it, as you still want the mixture to be thick. Allow to stand for at least 30 minutes.

3 Meanwhile, make the romesco. Toast the almonds in a dry frying pan over a medium heat for 2 minutes until golden. Tip into a food processor or blender, along with the rest of the romesco ingredients except the maple syrup, and blend until completely smooth. Season to taste; you may want to add the maple syrup if your peppers are a little bitter.

4 Preheat the oven to 200°C/180°F fan/400°F/gas mark 6.

5 Place a large frying pan over a medium heat and pour in enough oil to generously cover the base. Test a little nugget of the fritter mixture by frying it briefly to check the seasoning. Add more salt, if needed. Scoop heaped teaspoons of the fritter mixture into the frying pan and flatten gently. Cook for a couple of minutes on each side until browned, then transfer to a large, lined baking sheet. Repeat with the remaining batter to make about 20 fritters, then bake them for 5–10 minutes.

6 Serve the fritters warm or at room temperature, with the romesco for dipping

LEMONY BEAN DIP – 3 WAYS

White beans create a base that is so silky smooth, they don't need much else done to them, particularly when they are good quality. You can blitz them, mash them or braise them, then flavour with fresh lemon and garlic to create a trusty base that you can accessorise as you please (our top three suggestions are below). Everyone has their own zing tolerance, so adjust the lemon juice to taste. Any white beans will work in this recipe – haricot, cannellini or butter beans. Serve warm or cold.

Feeds 4 as a side
Takes 15 minutes

700g (1lb 9oz) jar white beans, or 1 White Bean Base (page 184), drained plus 1–2 tablespoons of bean stock

1 garlic clove, crushed

2 tablespoons olive oil

zest and juice of 2 lemons (use more or less to taste)

THE BASE

1 Add the beans or the bean base to a blender or food processor, along with the garlic, olive oil and lemon zest.

2 If serving cold: Add the lemon juice to the mixture and blitz until you reach a smooth consistency. Add a tablespoon or so of bean stock if you need to loosen it.

3 If serving warm: blitz the ingredients without the lemon juice, then add to a saucepan over a medium heat and warm through. If the mixture is too thick and catches on the bottom of the pan, add the bean stock. Once hot, remove from the heat and stir through the lemon juice to taste.

4 Spoon the dip on to a plate and choose your accessory opposite to dress with.

1 CRISPY SAGE DIP

Serve with neutral-tasting snacks such as pitta chips to allow the flavours to shine.

2 tablespoons olive oil

10–12 fresh sage leaves

1 quantity of Lemony Bean Dip (opposite)

1 Heat the oil in a small frying pan over a medium heat. When shimmering, add the sage leaves in a single layer. Watch them closely as it only takes about 30 seconds or so for them to crisp up, then remove them with a slotted spoon and place on a paper towel to drain.

2 Spoon the lemony dip into a serving bowl and sprinkle the crispy sage leaves over the top. Drizzle with the remaining sage oil from the pan to serve.

2 CRISPY CAPERS

Particularly good alongside fish and some steamed greens, but it also works well on olive-oil-seared bread.

2 tablespoons olive oil

1–2 tablespoons capers

1 quantity of Lemony Bean Dip (opposite)

1 Heat the oil in a small frying pan over a medium heat. Drain the capers and pat them dry with a paper towel (this ensures they don't splatter everywhere!). Add to the pan and cook for 4–5 minutes until crisp, stirring occasionally. Depending on how dry your capers are, they may need a bit longer for the pickling liquor to burn off. Using a slotted spoon, remove the capers from the pan and put onto a piece of paper towel to drain.

2 Spoon the lemony dip into a serving bowl and sprinkle the crispy capers over the top.

3 SALSA VERDE

Serve on crostini or load it up in a big wide dish and serve with crispbreads as more of a sharing feast.

1 quantity of Lemony Bean Dip (opposite)

1 quantity of Salsa Verde (page 44)

1 Simply spoon the lemony dip into a serving bowl and top with the salsa verde to serve.

Delicious, spicy-sweet carrots on a bed of creamy whipped feta. We'd serve this with some warm flatbreads. If you don't have carrot tops, use fresh parsley.

MOB'S HONEY HARISSA CARROTS WITH WHIPPED FETA

Feeds 4
Takes 40 minutes

500g (1lb 2oz) carrots with their tops (or 30g parsley), finely chopped

3 tablespoons olive oil

½ teaspoon ground cinnamon

juice of 1 lemon

300g (10½oz) thick Greek yogurt (or soured cream or crème fraîche)

150g (5½oz) feta

½ 700g (1lb 9oz) jar chickpeas, or 1 x 400g (14oz) can chickpeas, drained, rinsed and patted dry with paper towels

2 tablespoons honey (or agave or maple syrup)

2 tablespoons harissa paste

salt and freshly ground black pepper

bread, to serve

1 Preheat your oven to 190°C/170°C fan/375°F/gas mark 5.

2 Toss the carrots into a roasting tray, reserving the tops for the pesto. Drizzle with 1 tablespoon of the olive oil, then scatter over the cinnamon and a pinch of salt and pepper. Mix to combine, then roast for 30 minutes.

3 Meanwhile, add the carrot tops (about 2 tablespoons' worth) to a pestle and mortar, along with the lemon juice and the remaining olive oil. Bash together until you have a chunky green sauce.

4 Tip your yogurt into a medium-sized mixing bowl and finely crumble in your feta. Whisk until the feta has totally incorporated, then season to taste with salt and pepper.

5 Once the carrots have been roasting for 30 minutes, remove from the oven and tip the chickpeas into the roasting tray. Toss to combine, then return the tray to the oven for another 15 minutes until the carrots are roasted and the chickpeas are crisp.

6 Mix together your honey and harissa paste in a small bowl.

7 Remove the carrots and chickpeas from the oven. Pour the honey and harissa mixture over them and give them a toss until they are all coated.

8 Spoon your whipped feta yogurt on to a serving plate and top with your chickpeas and carrots. Drizzle with your carrot-top pesto, then serve and enjoy, with bread for dipping.

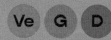

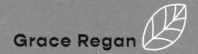

Grace Regan

This isn't a traditional chaat, but it contains all the flavour and texture components of a typical chaat. And believe me when I say it's a flavour party – one shovel of these fresh, saucy, crispy chickpeas into your mouth, and you won't be able to stop. The chutney packs a punch, and it's meant to, but rein in the salt depending on your preference. Don't be put off by the many stages in the recipe – it's very simple to assemble.

Feeds 4
Takes 40 minutes

CRISPY CHICKPEA CHAAT

For the pickled pink onion

1 large red onion, thinly sliced

½ teaspoon fine sea salt

juice of 1 lime

For the coriander chutney

100ml (3½fl oz) vegetable oil

5 garlic cloves

2 green chillies, stems removed

2 teaspoons white caster sugar

juice of 2 limes

3 tablespoons white wine vinegar

3 large bunches of coriander (about 30g/1oz each), stalks included

small bunch of flat-leaf parsley (about 15g/½oz), stalks included

For the raita

340g (12oz) silken tofu, drained (or the same weight of yogurt)

½ cucumber, roughly chopped

small bunch of mint leaves (about 15g/½oz)

½ teaspoon ground cumin

½ teaspoon freshly ground black pepper

juice of 1 lemon

1 Start by making the pickled pink onion. Put the onion into a small bowl and add the salt. Massage the salt into the onion and set aside for 20 minutes. In this time, the salt will draw the moisture out of the onion, and it will go soft and translucent.

2 While your onion is marinating in the salt, get your coriander chutney and raita prepared.

3 For the chutney, put all the ingredients, plus 1½ teaspoons fine sea salt, into a blender with 100ml (3½fl oz) water and blitz until a smooth chutney is formed. If you have a small blender, start by blending everything apart from the herbs, then slowly add the herbs, bit by bit. Decant into a container; this makes more than you need for this recipe, but it will last for up to 7 days in the fridge.

4 Now make the raita. Put all the ingredients, plus ½ teaspoon fine sea salt, into a blender or food processor and blitz until a smooth sauce is formed. Taste for seasoning – it may need a touch more lemon or salt. Again, you will have more than you will need for the chaat, so store in the fridge and eat within 5 days.

5 Back to the pink onion. Once it's had 20 minutes, add the lime juice and massage it in. Leave for 45 minutes–1 hour until the lime juice has turned the onion bright pink. This pickle will keep in the fridge for 2 weeks.

6 Now it's time to make the kachumber. Mix together all the ingredients, plus ½ teaspoon fine sea salt, in a bowl and taste for seasoning. This is best eaten fresh, so avoid preparing it too far in advance.

For the kachumber

2 tomatoes, finely diced

1 cucumber, deseeded and finely diced

small bunch of mint leaves (about 15g/½oz), finely chopped

small bunch of coriander (about 15g/½oz), finely chopped

½ teaspoon white caster sugar

¼ teaspoon freshly ground black pepper

juice of 1 lime

For the crispy chickpeas

3 tablespoons neutral oil

½ 700g jar chickpeas or 1 x 400g (14oz) can chickpeas, drained, rinsed and patted dry with paper towel

2 teaspoons ground cumin

1 teaspoon ground coriander

½ teaspoons ground cinnamon

To garnish

handful of fine sev (or shop-bought crispy onions if you can't find sev)

handful of finely chopped coriander

7 And finally, the star of the show: the crispy chickpeas. Heat the oil in a large frying pan over a medium heat. When it's smoking hot, add the chickpeas – if using canned, add a pinch of salt at this point – and fry until they begin to crisp up and turn golden brown. This will take around 8 minutes. Resist the temptation to stir them, as they get crispier if you leave them alone. Around halfway through cooking, give the pan a shake.

8 When the chickpeas are golden, take the pan off the heat and add the ground spices. Shake the pan well to make sure they are evenly coated. Pour the chickpeas on to a plate lined with paper towels, then sprinkle them with a teaspoon of salt. Leave to cool slightly – this is when they become extra crispy.

9 Now you're ready to assemble your chaat. Take out a large, flat serving dish and spoon on the kachumber as a base. Next add the crispy chickpeas, then drizzle over the raita, followed by the coriander chutney. Finish by sprinkling over a generous handful of sev, followed by the pickled pink onion and a handful of chopped coriander. Serve.

A dark, broody affair with black beans and black garlic. Like most people, we were introduced to this ingredient by Ottolenghi. The black garlic packs a load of smoky umami into the base of this dish, and the herby yogurt cuts through it all with a zingy beauty. We like to serve it with some crispbreads or toasted pitta and crudités for a real original dip.

BLACK GARLIC DIP WITH FETA + HERB YOGURT

Feeds 4 as an appetiser
Takes 15 minutes

For the black garlic dip

black garlic cloves from 1 bulb (35–40g/1¼–1½oz)

700g (1lb 9oz) jar black beans with 2 tablespoons of their bean stock reserved, or 2 × 400g (14oz) cans black beans

1 tablespoon extra virgin olive oil

½ teaspoon ground cumin (optional)

For the feta and herb yogurt

small bunch of basil (about 15g/½oz)

small bunch of parsley, leaves only (about 15g/½oz)

1 green or red chilli, deseeded and roughly chopped

½ teaspoon sea salt

2 tablespoons full-fat Greek yogurt or soured cream

1–2 tablespoons olive oil

50g (1¾oz) feta

juice of ½ lemon

To serve

60g (2¼oz) toasted sunflower or pumpkin seeds

crispbreads or toasted pitta

crudités of your choice

1 To make the dip, combine all the ingredients in a food processor and blend until smooth. If it's too thick at this point, add a spoonful of the bean stock (or water, if using canned) to loosen. Season to taste.

2 For the herbed yogurt, blitz together the ingredients in a food processor until smooth. Loosen with more olive oil if needed.

3 To assemble, spread the black bean dip across the base of a wide plate or pour into a bowl. Dot with the herby yogurt and sprinkle over the toasted seeds for crunch. Serve with crispbreads and crudités of your choice.

If you can't find black garlic, roast a bulb of garlic with olive oil and salt until soft, then add a few pinches of paprika for extra smokiness.

CRISPY CHICKPEAS – 3 WAYS

Crisping up chickpeas is a crucial technique in your bean-basics repertoire. They add texture to soups and stews, mimic croutons in salads and, in some cases, like our Chick-PLT (page 23), are a strong contender for replacing bacon. Patting dry the rinsed and drained chickpeas is one of the most important steps, so make sure you do it. If using smaller chickpeas, reduce the roasting time by 5 minutes.

Feeds 4 as a snack
Takes 20–25 minutes

700g (1lb 9oz) jar Queen Chickpeas, or 2 × 400g (14oz) cans chickpeas

THE CRISPY PREP

1   Preheat the oven to 220°C/200°C fan/425°F/gas mark 7.

2   Drain the chickpeas and rinse them to remove the sticky bean stock (this will help them dry out and crisp up).

3   Tumble on to a wide baking tray and pat dry with a paper towel to remove any remaining liquid. Make sure the chickpeas are spread out evenly in a single layer, avoiding contact with one another where possible.

4   If using canned chickpeas, check their salt level (it should say on the can), and scatter ½ teaspoon fine salt over the chickpeas if you think it is needed. Toss to coat.

5   Choose your flavouring combo opposite and proceed as instructed.

Serving ideas

Sage + Rosemary
• Use as a toast topper with juicy, charred tomatoes (page 44) and feta.
• Scatter over a whipped, lemony ricotta dip to add crunch, with pitta chips for dunking.
• Use as crunchy croutons for a winter veg soup, such as leek and potato.

Maple + Cinnamon
• Sprinkle on to yogurt or serve with pancakes for a fun brunch.
• Try as a sweet, crunchy topping with an autumnal veg salad or soup.

Chilli
• Use as a crunchy topping for your favourite curry.
• Use as a protein source in a burrito bowl.

SAGE + ROSEMARY
CRISPY CHICKPEAS

700g (1lb 9oz) jar Queen Chickpeas, or 2 × 400g (14oz) cans chickpeas

4–6 rosemary sprigs, leaves picked

20g (¾oz) fresh sage leaves, torn into strips (leave a few whole for decoration, if you like)

2–3 tablespoons olive oil

1 Do the crispy prep as instructed opposite.

2 Scatter the rosemary and sage into the tray. Drizzle the chickpeas with olive oil and toss to mix everything together. Roast for 25 minutes for Queen Chickpeas or 20 minutes for smaller chickpeas, stirring halfway through.

3 Being careful of the heat, taste a chickpea to see if they're ready. You want them to be crispy on the outside but soft in the middle. Cook for a further 5–10 minutes if they are a little soft. Once you're happy, remove from the oven.

MAPLE + CINNAMON
CRISPY CHICKPEAS

700g (1lb 9oz) jar Queen Chickpeas, or 2 × 400g (14oz) cans chickpeas

1 tablespoon olive oil

4 tablespoons maple syrup

1 teaspoon ground cinnamon

1 Do the crispy prep as instructed above, then put the chickpeas in the oven just as they are for 15 minutes or so to crisp up slightly.

2 Remove from the oven and drizzle over the olive oil and maple syrup, then sprinkle over the cinnamon and toss well to coat. Return to the oven for 10–12 minutes for Queen Chickpeas and 5–7 minutes for smaller chickpeas, until crispy and golden. You may need to toss halfway through to prevent the chickpeas from burning or sticking to the base of the pan.

CHILLI CRISPY
CHICKPEAS

700g (1lb 9oz) jar Queen Chickpeas, or 2 × 400g (14oz) cans chickpeas

2–3 tablespoons olive oil

1 teaspoon chilli powder

1 teaspoon smoked paprika

1 Do the crispy prep as instructed opposite, then drizzle over the olive oil and scatter over the chilli powder and smoked paprika. Toss well to coat.

2 Roast for 23–30 minutes for Queen Chickpeas or 18–25 minutes for smaller chickpeas, until crispy, tossing halfway through.

BIG BEANS
BEST

Hannah Wilding

This is one of our most popular recipes and was the first one I made with the Bold Bean Co team, so it holds a pretty special place in my heart! It can be served as a speedy weeknight dinner with a fresh side salad, or topped with roasted toms for a burst of sweetness and colour. We've used a classic basil pesto here, but if it's wild garlic season, use this in place of the garlic clovel. Opt for the biggest, fattest Queen butter beans you can get your hands on.

Feeds 2–3
Takes 10 minutes

700g (1lb 9oz) jar Queen Butter Beans, or 1 Butter Bean Base (page 184), with their bean stock if you like

250g (9oz) ricotta (or burrata or stracciatella cheese)

zest of 2 lemons, plus juice to taste

freshly ground black pepper

For the pesto
large handful of pine nuts, toasted (or walnuts)

large bunch of basil (about 30g/1oz)

1 garlic clove

good handful of grated vegetarian hard cheese or Parmesan (about 25g/1oz)

4–5 tablespoons olive oil, plus extra to serve

To serve
juicy charred tomatoes, to top (page 44), fresh rocket salad

RICOTTA + PESTO BUTTER BEANS

1 To make the pesto, add the pine nuts, basil, garlic and cheese to a blender or food processor, along with 4 tablespoons of the olive oil. Blitz until you have an oozy, purée-like consistency; you may need to add more oil to bind the mixture together. You could also try doing this in a pestle and mortar for a chunkier texture.

2 Next, prepare the butter beans. In winter, we like serving this as a brothy bean base, so we recommend saving some of the bean stock and warming through with the beans in a pan. For summer, we like it lighter, so simply drain and rinse the beans and don't bother to warm through.

3 Spoon the beans on to your serving plate and dollop over the ricotta. Drizzle over the pesto and scatter over the lemon zest, plus a small squeeze of the juice if you like a real zing! Finish with some cracked black pepper and a final drizzle of olive oil for extra indulgence.

If you're pressed for time, use shop-bought red or green pesto: it still makes a delicious dish.

 **Georgia Levy**

Crunching into one of these while it's hot is one of life's greatest pleasures. Falafels are usually made with dried chickpeas, but dried black beans work just as well and imbue a gentle, nutty creaminess which is perfectly offset by the tangy pomegranate salad and herby tahini dip. Canned beans aren't a great substitute, I'm afraid, so you'll need to remind yourself to soak them the night before.

Feeds 4 (makes 25–30)
Takes 1 hour

BLACK BEAN FALAFEL WITH GREEN TAHINI

1 large onion, roughly chopped

3 garlic cloves, roughly chopped

small bunch of parsley (about 15g/½oz), roughly chopped

½ small bunch of dill (about 10g/¼oz), roughly chopped

1½ teaspoons ground cumin

1½ teaspoons ground coriander

300g (10½oz) dried black beans, soaked overnight in cold water

1½ teaspoons sea salt, plus extra to taste

2 tablespoons gram or plain flour (use gram flour to make it gluten-free), plus extra if needed

1 teaspoon gluten-free or ordinary baking powder

sunflower oil, for frying

freshly ground black pepper

For the pomegranate chopped salad

1 cucumber, deseeded and cubed

300g (10½oz) cherry tomatoes, quartered

1 tablespoon pomegranate seeds

2 tablespoons olive oil

juice of ½ lemon

1 Pop the onion, garlic, herbs and spices into a food processor and blitz until coarsely chopped.

2 Drain the soaked beans and roughly dry them in a clean tea towel. Add to the food processor, along with the salt, flour and baking powder, and blitz again until everything is finely chopped.

3 Transfer to a mixing bowl. If you grab a handful of the mix, it should hold together. If not, add another tablespoon of flour. Pop this mixture into the fridge while you make the salad.

4 For the chopped salad, combine the cucumber, tomatoes and pomegranate seeds in a bowl, then drizzle over the oil. Don't toss or add the lemon juice and seasoning yet – we'll do this just before eating so everything stays crunchy. Set aside.

5 Make the green tahini dip next. Combine all the ingredients in a small jug, along with 4 tablespoons water. Use a handheld blender (or a small blender) to combine until bright green and smooth. Season to taste.

6 Line a plate or tray with paper towels. Set a large, heavy-based pan, ideally a wok, over a high heat, and pour in oil to a depth of 3cm (1¼in). Heat the oil to about 160–180°C (320–356°F). If you don't have a thermometer, a good way to test the oil temperature is by chucking in a piece of bread; if it browns within 20 seconds, you're good to go. Using two tablespoons, shape 1 heaped tablespoon of the mix into a round-ish ball and very carefully slide into the hot oil. Repeat with the remaining mixture, working in batches so you don't overcrowd the pan.

7 Cook each batch for 3–4 minutes, making sure you roll the balls over to cook on all sides. Once they are dark golden and crisp, scoop out of

For the green tahini dip

1 garlic clove, roughly chopped

2 big handfuls of chopped parsley

100g (3½oz) tahini

juice of 1 lemon

2 tablespoons olive oil

the pan and place on the paper towels to drain while you cook the rest. Maybe break open one to check that the inside is nicely cooked. If not, your oil may be a little too hot, in which case switch off the heat and leave for a few minutes before continuing to fry.

8 To serve, squeeze the lemon over the salad, season and toss, then serve immediately with the falafels and tahini dip and some flatbreads.

BROTHY BEANS 3

For best results, the parsnips, pears and onion should all be chopped into similar 2cm (¾in) chunks. When roasted in their skins, the garlic cloves deliver a sweet but rounded depth that we LOVE and the nutty rosemary pesto makes it even more flavoursome. If you don't have time to make pesto, use shop-bought and stir through 1 tablespoon fresh or dried rosemary just before serving.

WHITE BEAN SOUP WITH HAZELNUT ROSEMARY PESTO

Feeds 3
Takes 45–50 minutes

3 medium or 2 large parsnips, peeled and roughly chopped

2 pears, peeled and roughly chopped

1 large onion, roughly chopped

3–4 fat garlic cloves, skin on

2 tablespoons extra virgin olive oil

1 teaspoon ground cumin (optional)

700g (1lb 9oz) jar white beans with their bean stock, or 2 × 400g (14oz) can white beans with 200ml (7fl oz) veg or chicken stock

about 450ml (15fl oz) vegetable or chicken stock

sea salt and freshly ground black pepper

For the pesto
small bunch of parsley (about 15g/½oz), roughly chopped

4 tablespoons extra virgin olive oil

1 tablespoon finely chopped rosemary leaves (or sage fried in olive oil until crispy)

50g (1¾oz) blanched and toasted hazelnuts (or walnuts or pine nuts)

50g (1¾oz) vegetarian hard cheese or Parmesan, or Pecorino, grated

1 Preheat the oven to 200°C/180°C/400°F/gas mark 6 and line a roasting tray with foil.

2 Tumble the chopped parsnips, pears, onion and whole garlic cloves (skin on) onto the roasting tray. Drizzle generously with olive oil and season with the cumin, salt and pepper and give it a good mix. Roast for 35–40 minutes until the vegetables are tender and have started to caramelise.

3 While the veg are roasting, make the hazelnut and rosemary pesto. Combine all the pesto ingredients in a blender and blitz until a chunky paste is formed. Alternatively, grind the ingredients in a pestle and mortar for an even chunkier texture. Season to taste. Add more olive oil to loosen if necessary.

4 Remove the roasting tray from the oven. Squeeze the garlic out of its skins and tip the contents of the tray into a large, deep pan. Add the beans with their bean stock, along with the additional stock, and blitz until smooth using a handheld blender. How much additional stock you add will depend on the consistency you like your soup. Heat the soup through until hot.

5 To serve, pour the hot soup into warm bowls. Top each one with a spoonful of the pesto. This soup can happily be made in advance (it will keep for up to 3 days) and can be reheated in a saucepan to serve. It will also freeze well; cook straight from frozen until piping hot.

This sunny recipe, taken from Anna Jones' book *A Modern Way to Eat,* is as good for breakfast as it is for dinner. It's a soupy stew that's great on its own, but you can take it to the next level by topping it with popping roasted tomatoes, buttery avocado and even a perfectly poached egg. A serious team of flavours in a bowl.

SWEET POTATO + BLACK BEAN TORTILLA BOWLS

Feeds 4
Takes 35–40 minutes

1 sweet potato, washed and chopped into small chunks

200g (7oz) cherry tomatoes, halved

2 tablespoons olive oil, plus extra for drizzling

bunch of spring onions, finely sliced (or 1 large red onion, finely diced)

2 garlic cloves, finely sliced

1 teaspoon sweet smoked paprika

1 teaspoon ground coriander

1 teaspoon ground cumin

1 teaspoon ground cinnamon

400g (14oz) can chopped tomatoes

550ml (18½fl oz) hot vegetable stock

700g (1lb 9oz) jar black beans with their bean stock, or 2 × 400g (14oz) cans black beans with 200ml (7fl oz) veg stock

6 corn or wheat tortillas, sliced into 5mm (¼in) strips (or nachos sprinkled over at the end)

sea salt and freshly ground black pepper

1 Preheat your oven to 200°C/180°C fan/400°F/gas mark 6.

2 Arrange the sweet potato chunks on one side of a baking tray and the halved cherry tomatoes on the other. Season both with some salt and pepper, then drizzle with 1 tablespoon of the olive oil and toss to coat, but try to keep the tomatoes and sweet potatoes separate. Roast for 20–25 minutes.

3 Meanwhile, heat the remaining 1 tablespoon of olive oil in a large saucepan over a medium heat. Add the spring onions and garlic and sizzle for a few minutes until the garlic has just started to brown, then add all the spices and stir a couple of times. Add the canned tomatoes and simmer for 5 minutes, until all the flavours have come together.

4 Add the stock and bring to the boil, then simmer for another 5 minutes. I like to blitz the broth at this point, but feel free to skip this if you like more texture.

5 Add the beans with their bean or veg stock. If you like, you could mush a few of the beans in your hands as you add them (it can get messy, but it's worth it!) to add texture.

6 By now, the tomatoes and sweet potatoes should be roasted, so remove the tray from the oven (but leave the oven on). Add the sweet potatoes to the broth and keep it ticking over on a low heat. Set the roasted tomatoes aside – they will go in later.

7 Arrange the tortilla strips on a large baking tray. Season with a little salt and drizzle over some oil, then toss to coat. Bake in the oven for 4–5 minutes until crisp and lightly golden.

To serve

4 eggs (optional)

1 avocado, cut into chunks

Greek yogurt or soured cream

small bunch of coriander (about 15g/½oz), leaves picked

8 I like to serve poached eggs on top of my soup, so if you like this idea, poach the eggs to your liking.

9 Once the tortilla strips are golden, take them out of the oven. Ladle the soup into bowls and top with the roasted tomatoes and crunchy tortilla strips. Top each one with a poached egg (if using), some chopped avocado, a dollop of yogurt or soured cream and a scattering of coriander.

We describe this soup as 'zippy': zippy to make, zippy to taste. Inspired by what the Lithuanians call 'pink soup', it's easier to make than gazpacho and, with the numerous textural layers going on, brings far more to the party, in our opinion. The hot buttered beans add a richness to a fresh, clean-feeling meal. By alternating mouthfuls, you're able to appreciate both elements in their own right, and eating them together can feel like magic.

BEETROOT GAZPACHO WITH BROWN BUTTER BLACK BEANS

Feeds 3
Takes 20 minutes

½ cucumber (about 150g/5½oz), roughly chopped into bite-sized chunks

300g (10½oz) vacuum-packed beetroot, with the juices, roughly chopped

small bunch of dill (about 15g/½oz), finely chopped

4 spring onions, finely chopped

500ml (17fl oz) kefir or yogurt, cold

1 teaspoon horseradish (optional)

sea salt and freshly ground black pepper

For the beans

40g (1½oz) butter

½ 700g (1lb 9oz) jar black beans, or 400g (14oz) can black beans, drained and rinsed

1 In a food processor or blender, combine the cucumber and beetroot, a quarter of the dill, and half the spring onions, reserving the whitest parts for the beans. Pour in the fridge-cold kefir or yogurt and season with salt and pepper. You can add the horseradish here if you want it super-zingy, but the fresh spring onions should give some zing on their own. Blitz until smooth.

2 To make the beans, melt the butter in a heavy-based saucepan over a medium heat. Once it has melted, it will begin to bubble. Let this happen until the water has cooked off and the butter begins to smell nutty and turn brown. At this point, add the reserved spring onions to the pan, along with the black beans. Tilt the pan a little and swirl the butter through the beans. Take off the heat and stir through half the dill. Season to taste.

3 To serve, pour the smooth, cold beetroot soup into bowls, scatter over the remaining dill and serve alongside a bowl of the warm black beans. We recommend scooping warm spoonfuls of the beans into the broth, then consuming immediately so that the butter doesn't harden and you get the stunning hot–cold, fresh creamy contrast between the two.

This is an incredibly easy stew, packed full of veggies, that you can whip up for a quick supper that feels almost festive. It is rich and full of flavour, with a lovely heat to it.

SWEET + SPICY SQUASH + CHICKPEA STEW

Feeds 4
Takes 30–35 minutes

2 teaspoons cumin seeds

3 tablespoons olive oil

2 leeks, roughly sliced

3 garlic cloves, chopped

2 red or green chillies, finely chopped

5 sprigs of oregano or thyme, leaves chopped

1 butternut squash, skin on, deseeded and chopped into 2.5cm (1in) pieces (or 2 sweet potatoes)

1 cinnamon stick

1 bay leaf (fresh or dried)

400–600ml (14–20fl oz) veg stock

700g (1lb 9oz) jar chickpeas with their bean stock, or 2 × 400g (14oz) cans chickpeas with 200ml (7fl oz) extra veg stock

200g (7oz) chard, cavolo nero or spring greens, roughly chopped

sea salt and ground black pepper

To serve (optional)

100g (3½oz) Lancashire cheese, grated (or a mild Cheddar or Wensleydale)

50g (1¾oz) toasted seeds of your choice (we like pumpkin or sunflower)

chilli oil

Greek yogurt or soured cream

sourdough bread

1   Toast the cumin seeds in large, high-sided dry frying pan (we'll use this pan again later), then grind in a pestle and mortar or spice grinder (if you have a food processor, this works too!).

2   Heat the olive oil in the same pan over a medium heat. Add the leeks and cook for 5 minutes until tender, then add the garlic, chillies, oregano or thyme, along with the toasted cumin seeds. Cook for a further 3 minutes.

3   Add the diced squash, along with the cinnamon stick and bay leaf, and stir. Pour over 400ml (14fl oz) of the stock (throw in the bean stock, too, if using jarred, or the extra 200ml (7fl oz) veg stock if using canned) and bring to the boil, then reduce the heat to a simmer. Cook for about 20 minutes, or until the squash is soft but not falling apart. Top up with extra veg stock if looking too dry.

4   Add the chickpeas and greens and season to taste, then bubble away for a further 3–4 minutes if you're using jarred beans, and 8–10 minutes if using canned, to allow the beans to reach a softer texture.

5   When it's ready, divide between serving bowls and sprinkle over the grated cheese and seeds. Drizzle each portion with chilli oil, then serve with dollops of Greek yogurt and some sourdough bread.

For crunch, try topping with our Maple + Cinnamon Crispy Chickpeas (page 75)

This is the sort of warming, bolstering bowl that carries you through the coldest days of the year. Generous servings of ginger and fresh turmeric give warmth to the base, while the juicy squirts of lemon and generous handfuls of herbs provide freshness to finish.

GOLDEN CHICKPEA + LEMON SOUP WITH STICKY SHALLOTS

Feeds 4
Takes 30–35 minutes

5 banana shallots, finely sliced

5 tablespoons olive oil

3 garlic cloves, finely grated

7.5cm (3in) piece of fresh ginger, finely grated

5cm (2in) piece of fresh turmeric, finely grated (or 1 teaspoon ground turmeric)

700g (1lb 9oz) jar chickpeas, or 1 Chickpea Base (page 184)

400ml (14fl oz) can full-fat coconut milk

400ml (14fl oz) veg stock or water

juice of 1 lemon

sea salt and freshly ground black pepper

To serve

natural yogurt or coconut yogurt

1 lemon, zested and cut into wedges

4 large handfuls of soft herbs (roughly 10g/¼oz each), such as parsley, coriander, mint or dill, leaves picked

1 Add the sliced shallots, olive oil and a really good pinch of salt to a cold, heavy-based saucepan. Set over a low–medium heat and cook, stirring regularly, for 20 minutes until deeply golden and sticky. Reduce the heat if needed and stir constantly for the last 5 minutes, as they can turn quite quickly.

2 Once the shallots are golden and sticky, scoop out half and transfer to a plate lined with paper towels.

3 Add the garlic, ginger and turmeric to the remaining shallots in the pan and fry for 1 minute, then add the chickpeas (including all their bean stock), along with the coconut milk and veg stock or water. Bring to a lively simmer and cook for 10 minutes until slightly thickened.

4 Stir through the lemon juice, season to taste and spoon into bowls. Serve topped with a dollop of yogurt, the reserved shallots, the lemon zest and soft herb, with lemon wedges on the side for squeezing.

The lemony flavours give this real freshness, making it a stew fit for summer as well as winter. You can sub in any other greens, depending on the season – asparagus, kale, green beans. It's a showstopper in itself, but if you wanted to serve it as a side, it would go beautifully with grilled white fish.

LEMON + HERBY BEAN BROTH WITH SEASONAL GREENS

Feeds 3–4
Takes 30 minutes

2 tablespoons olive oil, plus extra to serve

1 large onion, very finely chopped

3 large garlic cloves, thinly sliced

zest and juice of 1 large lemon

3 thyme sprigs, or ½ teaspoon dried thyme

pinch of dried chilli flakes

3 bay leaves (fresh or dried)

700g (1lb 9oz) jar white beans with their bean stock, or 2 × 400g (14oz) cans white beans with 200ml (7fl oz) veg stock

about 300ml (10fl oz) veg stock

150g (5½oz) spinach leaves, coarse stems discarded

100g (3½oz) frozen peas

100g (3½oz) long-stem broccoli

good handful of mint, leaves picked (about 10g/¼oz)

small handful of chives, finely sliced (about 10g/¼oz)

handful of flat-leaf parsley, leaves chopped (20g/¾oz)

handful of dill, chopped (about 20g/¾oz)

sea salt and freshly ground black pepper

1 Heat the olive oil in a large, heavy-based saucepan over a medium heat. Once hot, add the onion, garlic, lemon zest, thyme sprigs, chilli flakes and bay leaves, and season lightly with salt and pepper. Cook for 8–10 minutes, stirring regularly, not letting anything catch on the base of the pan.

2 Once everything is soft and fragrant, add the beans and their stock, along with the extra veg stock. Reduce the heat to low and bubble away for 4–5 minutes if using jarred beans; if using canned, add an extra pinch of salt and simmer for 10–13 minutes to allow the beans to soften a little more.

3 Add the spinach leaves to the pan and stir until wilted. Add the peas and broccoli, along with any other seasonal greens you're using. Let everything settle.

4 Chop half the mint leaves and add them to the beans, along with all of the chives, parsley, dill and lemon juice. Season to taste.

5 Ladle the beans into bowls and serve with a drizzle of olive oil and the remaining mint. This broth is delicious with a dollop of crème fraîche and bread for mopping up the sauce.

If you like, you could serve this sprinkled with crispy breadcrumbs for a bit of crunch.

Feeds 3–4
Takes 45 minutes

For the curry paste

4 tablespoons neutral oil

thumb-sized piece of ginger (50g/1¾oz), peeled and roughly chopped

2 garlic cloves, peeled

1 heaped teaspoon ground turmeric

4 spring onions, roughly chopped

1–2 small green chillies

small bunch of coriander (15g/½oz)

4–5 mint sprigs, leaves picked

For the broth

2 × 400ml (14fl oz) cans coconut milk

1 veggie stock cube, crumbled

1 tablespoon soy sauce or tamari

1 lemongrass stalk

700g (1lb 9oz) jar black beans with their bean stock, or 2 × 400g (14oz) cans black beans, drained

2 red or romano peppers, cut into 2.5cm (1in) strips

200g (7oz) mangetout, sliced into bite-sized pieces (or fine green beans or sliced courgettes)

300g (10½oz) quick-cook noodles

juice of 2 limes

maple syrup, to taste, if needed

shop-bought crispy onions, to serve (optional)

Making a homemade curry paste fresh is far easier than you might think, and it makes a world of difference in this recipe. We learned this trick from the veg queen, Anna Jones. Sometimes curries can be heavy and rich, but the blitzing of the fresh herbs really brings a lightness to this broth. (Of course, you can cheat and use a Thai green curry paste for something similar.) The balance of creamy coconut, fresh lime, sweet vegetables and earthy black beans makes this a super-satisfying, take on a Thai green.

BLACK BEAN, COCONUT + LEMONGRASS BROTH

1   Combine all of the ingredients for the curry paste in a food processor and blitz to combine.

2   Spoon the mixture into a large, heavy-based casserole dish or a large saucepan over a medium–high heat and warmth through, stirring for a minute. Add the coconut milk, stock cube and soy or tamari. Bash the lemongrass stalk using a rolling pin or jar of beans and add that to the pan as well.

3   Add the beans, along with 1 tablespoon of their stock (or water, if using canned) and the red pepper. Let this bubble away for 8–10 minutes until the pepper is tender. Finally, add the mangetout and bubble away for about 4 minutes until cooked, adding the quick-cook noodles for the last minute. Finish by adding lime juice to taste. You can add a squeeze of maple at this point if the curry needs some sweetness, or some more soy if it needs more salt.

4   Serve in big wide bowls and top with crispy onions, if using.

If you have any bread going stale, crumble this up and add it to the broth once the greens have wilted for added heartiness. A great way to avoid food waste!

We were introduced to the dish Ash Reshteh on the Instagram account of food stylist Jodie Nixon, and immediately got into the kitchen to craft our own version. We've used chickpeas to provide a base of savoury, nutty deliciousness, topped with contrasting crispy, caramelised onions, cooling yogurt and a fragrant sizzling mint oil, creating a dish that is bursting with flavour and texture. Ideal for serving with warm flatbreads, rice or bulgur wheat for something more filling. If you don't want to make the mint oil, sprinkle over freshly chopped mint before serving.

Feeds 2–3
Takes 40–45 minutes

PERSIAN-STYLE HERBY CHICKPEAS

2–4 tablespoons olive oil, plus extra if needed

1 tablespoon butter (optional)

2 onions, finely sliced

3 garlic cloves, crushed

1 teaspoon ground turmeric

½ teaspoon ground cumin

700g (1lb 9oz) jar chickpeas with their bean stock, or 2 × 400g (14oz) cans chickpeas with 200ml (7fl oz) veg stock

30g (1oz) coriander, finely chopped

30g (1oz) parsley, finely chopped

20g (¾oz) dill, finely chopped

150g (5½oz) spinach

juice of 1–2 lemons

sea salt and freshly ground black pepper

For the sizzling mint oil

1 tablespoon olive oil

2 tablespoons dried mint

To serve

4 tablespoons Greek or natural yogurt

50g (1¾oz) toasted flaked almonds (optional)

1 Heat 2 tablespoons of the olive oil and the butter (if using) in a large saucepan over a medium heat. If you're not using butter, add the remaining 2 tablespoons olive oil instead. Allow the butter to melt slightly, then add the onion. Cook for 15–20 minutes, without stirring too frequently, so they get nicely frizzled. Once crispy, transfer a quarter of the onions to a small bowl using a slotted spoon and set aside for topping.

2 Add the crushed garlic to the remaining onion in the pan and cook for 1 minute. Add a little more oil if your pan is a little dry.

3 Add the turmeric and cumin and stir to combine, then pour in the chickpeas, along with their bean or veg stock. If using jarred chickpeas, move on to the next step. If using canned, reduce the heat to low and gently simmer for 10–15 minutes, topping up with a tablespoon of stock if needed. You'll also need to check more thoroughly for seasoning.

4 Now add the coriander, dill, parsley and spinach, and cook until the greens have wilted – roughly 4–5 minutes – stirring regularly. Add the lemon juice (just use 1 lemon if you're not much of a citrus-lover) and season with salt and pepper. Simmer until the texture is to your liking.

5 For the sizzling mint oil, heat the oil in a frying pan over a medium heat. Add the dried mint and let it sizzle away for about 1 minute until fragrant, stirring frequently so it doesn't burn.

6 Divide the stew into bowls. Dollop over some yogurt, then top with the reserved frizzled onions and a sprinkling of toasted almonds, if using. Finish with a drizzle of sizzling mint oil and serve with bulgur wheat or flatbreads.

Xanthe Gladstone

This fresh and easy lunch recipe is perfect for when you have lots of veg to use up. If you don't have the veg specified here, replace them with whatever you've got; it's really just the base that's important. I would recommend using the highest-quality vegetable stock you can as you'll be rewarded by the flavour of the final dish. I love the punch that the ginger and garlic bring; they make it beautifully thirst-quenching.

Feeds 2–3
Takes 30 minutes

2–3 garlic cloves, finely grated

thumb-sized piece of fresh ginger, finely grated

800ml (1½ pints) hot vegetable stock

200g (7oz) cherry tomatoes

1 corn on the cob, kernels removed (or a 200g (7oz) can sweetcorn, drained)

200g (7oz) cavolo nero, stalks removed, roughly chopped (or kale, spinach or spring greens)

700g (1lb 9oz) jar white beans with their bean stock, or 2 × 400g (14oz) cans white bean with 200ml (7fl oz) veg stock

small handful (about 10g/¼oz) roughly chopped fennel fronds (or fresh dill)

juice of ½ lemon

sea salt and freshly ground black pepper

sourdough or crusty bread, to serve

SUMMER BEAN BROTH

1   Combine the garlic, ginger and vegetable stock in a saucepan over a medium heat. Let this simmer for about 10–15 minutes until the garlic and ginger have really infused through the liquid and it smells fragrant.

2   Add the cherry tomatoes and sweetcorn, and season with a pinch of salt. Let the tomatoes cook for about 5 minutes, then add the cavolo and the white beans with their bean stock. If using unsalted canned beans, add some extra seasoning here, too. Reduce the heat to low, cover with a lid, and leave to simmer until the cavolo nero has wilted. Squeeze in the lemon and season again, if it needs it.

3   Take the broth off the heat and divide between 2 bowls. Sprinkle the fennel fronds over the top and serve with a good hunk of bread.

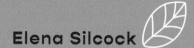
Elena Silcock

I wanted to call this dish 'let's play cards and eat spicy chickpeas', because this is the dish I cook when playing cards with my mates. It's THE ideal meal for when you want to be chilled and maybe a little lazy, but also to serve something filling. For ease, instead of roasting and peeling fresh peppers, you can use a jar of roasted jarred peppers.

Feeds 3
Takes 40 minutes

1 tablespoon olive oil, plus extra to serve

1 onion, finely sliced

2 garlic cloves, finely sliced

1 teaspoon fennel seeds

1 teaspoon dried oregano

1 tablespoon harissa paste (or 1 tablespoon tomato purée plus a big pinch of chilli flakes)

100ml (3½fl oz) white wine

200g (7oz) cherry tomatoes

700g (1lb 9oz) jar Queen Chickpeas, or 1 Chickpea Base (page 184)

400ml (14fl oz) veg stock

3 red peppers (or 3 roasted red peppers from a jar, drained and sliced)

juice of 1 lemon

150ml (5fl oz) natural or Greek yogurt or a dairy-free alternative

sea salt and freshly ground black pepper

To serve

smoked almonds or roasted salted almonds

freshly chopped parsley

SPICY RED PEPPER + CHICKPEA STEW

1 If using fresh peppers, set the grill to high.

2 Heat the oil in a frying pan over a medium–high heat. Add the onion, along with a big pinch of salt. Fry for 5–10 minutes, stirring regularly, until softened. Add the garlic, along with the fennel seeds, and toast for 2 minutes further. Stir in the oregano and harissa paste, then pour in the wine. Bubble away until reduced by half.

3 Add the tomatoes and poke their skins with a knife to make them burst. Cook, stirring, for 1 minute, then tip in the chickpeas, along with any stock from the jar, or the chickpea base. Add the vegetable stock, then reduce the heat to a simmer and leave to bubble for 25–30 minutes, stirring regularly. Add a little more water if it sticks at all.

4 If you're using fresh red peppers, put the red peppers on a baking tray and slide under the grill. Once they start to blacken, turn them over until they're charred on all sides. (You can also do this on a barbecue or over a gas stove: just char them straight on the flame, turning with tongs.) Once charred, place the peppers into a bowl and cover with clingfilm. Steaming them like this makes them super-easy to peel.

5 Once they're cool enough to handle, peel and discard the charred skins from the peppers, then roughly chop and add the soft peppers to the chickpeas. If using jarred red peppers, simply add them to the chickpeas now.

6 In a bowl, mix half the lemon juice with the yogurt and season well.

7 Taste the chickpeas. Add the remaining lemon juice and season well, then remove from the heat. Spoon into bowls and serve topped with yogurt, smoked almonds and parsley.

Sophie Godwin

We make a version of this pretty much once a week. Nothing beats the joy of a veggie one pot, and this – caramelised fennel and aubergine in a rich, garlicky tomato sauce with creamy butter beans – is a winner. The tangy caper vinaigrette cuts through everything, and of course, if I were you, I'd top it with a mountain of Parmesan.

AUBERGINE, FENNEL + TOMATO BUTTER BEANS

Feeds 2–3
Takes 40 minutes

1 tablespoon olive oil

1 fennel bulb, finely sliced

½ red onion, finely sliced (use the other ½ in the vinaigrette below)

1 large aubergine, cut into roughly 2cm (¾in) cubes

4 fat garlic cloves, finely sliced

2 teaspoons fennel seeds

big pinch of dried chilli flakes (optional)

400g (14oz) can cherry tomatoes or plum tomatoes

700g (1lb 9oz) jar Queen Butter Beans or 1 White Bean Base (page 184), with their bean stock

sea salt and freshly ground black pepper

For the caper vinaigrette

½ red onion, finely chopped

2 tablespoons capers

1–2 tablespoons sherry vinegar or red wine vinegar

3 tablespoons olive oil

To serve

vegetarian hard cheese or Parmesan, grated (save the rind, if you have it)

small bunch of basil leaves (about 15g/½oz)

1   Heat the oil in a large saucepan over a medium–high heat. Add the fennel and sliced red onion, along with a big pinch of salt. Cook, stirring regularly, for 5 minutes, then add the aubergine. Cook for a further 10 minutes until all the veg has collapsed and softened and is a little caramelised.

2   Scrape in the garlic and fennel seeds, along with the chilli flakes, if using, and cook for 1 minute more, then tip in the tomatoes. Half-fill the can with water, and pour that in too. Tip in your beans, along with their bean stock (this thickens the sauce). Chuck in a Parmesan rind, if you have one. Leave to bubble away for 10–15 minutes while you make the vinaigrette.

3   In a small bowl, mix the chopped red onion with the capers and vinegar. Add the olive oil and season to taste – iyou want the dish to be tangy, so add some more vinegar if needed.

4   Season the stew to taste, then ladle into bowls. Serve topped with the caper vinaigrette, grated Parmesan and basil leaves.

BEAN BOWLS 4

We all love a risotto, but say hello to the newest girl in town: bean-otto. Here, the creaminess of the white beans creates a base that's similar to a traditional risotto. The goat's cheese almost oozes into this soft and creamy bean bowl, and with the crispy sage gremolata on top, you have a killer combo you'll come back to time after time. It all really comes down to texture – before adding your beans, taste one and note how hard or soft the bean is. Adjust the cooking time accordingly. If you can, use a heritage squash such as delica or acorn – you'll really notice the difference.

WINTER SQUASH, SAGE + GOAT'S CHEESE BEAN-OTTO

Feeds 2–3
Takes 45–50 minutes

1 large butternut squash (about 900g/2lb), chopped into medium-sized chunks (see Tip overleaf) (or a small pumpkin)

2 tablespoons olive oil

1 onion or 2 banana shallots, finely diced

2 garlic cloves, crushed

700g (1lb 9oz) jar white beans with their bean stock, or 2 × 400g (14oz) cans white beans, drained, with 200ml (7fl oz) veg stock

150ml (5fl oz) white wine

20g (¾oz) salted butter

150g (5½oz) goat's cheese, crumbled, (or Boursin for something softer, gorgonzola for something punchier, or Brie)

sea salt and freshly ground black pepper

For the pine nut + crispy sage gremolata

50g (1¾oz) pine nuts (or walnuts)

2 tablespoons olive oil

20g (¾oz) fresh sage, roughly chopped

1 lemon, zested then cut into 4 wedges

1 Preheat the oven to 180°C/160°C fan/350°F/gas mark 4.

2 Toss the squash in a roasting tray with the olive oil and some salt and pepper. Roast for 35–40 minutes until caramelised, stirring halfway through to prevent the squash sticking to the tray.

3 Meanwhile, make the gremolata. Heat a large, deep frying pan or casserole dish over a medium heat and toast the pine nuts until starting to brown, then remove and set aside in a small bowl. Add the olive oil to the pan and, once hot, add the chopped sage. Fry for 30–50 seconds until crispy, then remove using a slotted spoon and add to the bowl with the pine nuts. Stir through the lemon zest and set aside.

4 Return the pan to the heat and add the onion to the hot sage oil still in the pan. Sauté for 8–10 minutes until softened, then add the garlic and cook for a further minute, or until fragrant.

5 Add the wine at this point and stir until it has reduced and the alchohol has burned off, which takes about 5 minutes. Then add the beans with their bean stock (or extra veg stock if using canned). If its looking too thick, loosen with a little water and continue bubbling. Remove from heat until the squash is ready.

CONTINUED OVERLEAF

6 Once the squash is cooked, remove from the oven. Put half of the squash chunks into a food processor with 1 tablespoon water to loosen into a thick purée. Alternatively, mash the squash with a fork; this takes less time and saves on washing-up! Return the remaining half of the squash chunks to the oven to crisp up even more for added texture.

7 Stir the squash purée through the beans and allow to heat through for a few minutes.

8 The bean-otto mixture should have reached a creamy consistency similar to that of a risotto; if it's still a little watery, let it bubble away for a few minutes more to thicken. Equally, add a splash of water if it needs loosening. Melt in the butter to give the bean-otto some shine, then top with the squash that has been roasting for a little longer.

9 Divide the bean-otto between bowls. Scatter over the goat's cheese and sprinkle over the pine nut gremolata. Serve with the lemon wedges for squeezing.

You can roast the squash skin on but peel it if you want a softer texture. For a great food-waste hack, toss the seeds in with the squash chunks and roast them until super-crispy, then sprinkle on top at the end for a good bit of crunch.

The 'BBBB', aka the ultimate start to your day. If you knew you were going to wake up to this bowl of goodness, trust us when we tell you that you'd wake up excited. Telling you how to fry an egg might sound silly, but if you use this method, you'll get the crispiest, frilliest egg of all time, which contrasts beautifully with the soft, oozy beans and avocado.

BBBB (BLACK BEAN BREAKFAST BOWLS FT. CRISPY FRIED EGG)

Feeds 2
Takes 20 minutes

3 tablespoons olive oil

½ onion, finely chopped

1 small garlic clove, crushed

50g (1¾oz) kale or 100g (3½oz) spinach, stems removed

700g (1lb 9oz) jar black beans with their bean stock, or 2 × 400g (14oz) cans black beans with 200ml (7fl oz) veg stock

2 eggs

1 perfectly ripe avocado, sliced

small handful of chives or coriander, chopped

sea salt and freshly ground black pepper

hot sauce, such as sriracha, to serve

1 Heat 1 tablespoon of the oil in a small saucepan over a medium heat. Add the onion, along with a pinch of salt, and cook slowly for 6–8 minutes until softened. Add the garlic and cook for another minute.

2 Meanwhile, put the kale or spinach into a big heat-proof bowl and pour over boiling water so that the leaves are fully submerged. Leave for 4–5 minutes, then drain.

3 Add the beans and stock to the onion and garlic mixture, breaking up the beans with your hands as you pour them in to thicken the sauce. Simmer for 5 minutes if using jarred beans, or 13–15 minutes if using canned, as they'll need to soften a little. Stir through the kale or spinach and season with black pepper. You may want to add a few more tablespoons of stock or some water at this point: you want the mixture to be the consistency of thick porridge. Taste and add more salt if needed.

4 Now, fry your eggs. Heat the remaining oil in a heavy-based frying pan over a medium–high heat until it shimmers. Crack the eggs carefully into the hot oil and season with salt and pepper. Tilt the pan slightly towards you so the oil creates a little pool at the front of the pan. Using a spoon, baste the eggs with the hot oil, aiming at the uncooked portions of the egg whites and avoiding the yolk. Continue basting until the eggs are puffy and cooked; this will take 45 seconds–1 minute. Transfer to a plate.

5 To serve, tumble the black bean mixture into 2 bowls, then top with the eggs and avocado slices. Scatter over the chives or coriander, drizzle with hot sauce, and enjoy.

Ultra-comforting creamed corn is a southern US classic, often served as a side at barbecues. We've made it the main event by dressing it with a zingy salsa and topping it with a load of smoky red beans, which pop as they are crisped up. We love the soft, porridge-like texture of this creamy corn with the crispy beans. Eat on its own, or with some griddled Baby Gem lettuce. You can use either canned for frozen sweetcorn.

CRISPY BEANS WITH CREAMED CORN + JALAPEÑO SALSA

Feeds 2
Takes 50 minutes–1 hour

For the crispy beans

700g (1lb 9oz) jar red beans, or 2 × 400g (14oz) cans red kidney beans, drained (or black beans)

1 tablespoon olive oil

1 tablespoon smoked paprika

sea salt and freshly ground black pepper

For the creamed corn

50g (1¾oz) salted butter

600g (1lb 5oz) sweetcorn kernels

2 garlic cloves, peeled

200ml (7fl oz) whole milk

3 spring onions, finely chopped

70g (2½oz) mature Cheddar (or other strong cheese), grated

For the jalapeño salsa

zest and juice of ½ lemon

20g (¾oz) pickled jalapeños, plus 1 tablespoon pickling juice

60g (2¼oz) extra virgin olive oil

pinch of sea salt

squeeze of honey or agave

30g (1oz) coriander, roughly chopped

10g (¼oz) mint leaves

1   Preheat the oven to 200°C/180°C fan/400°F/gas mark 6. Rinse your beans and pat dry with a paper towel; this helps them crisp up. Mix with the olive oil, paprika and a good pinch of salt, and spread them out on a large baking tray, giving them as much space as possible. Roast in the oven for 20 minutes, until the beans have popped and are beginning to colour. Remove from the oven, but leave it on.

2   While the beans are roasting, make the creamed corn. Melt the butter in a heavy-based saucepan over a medium–high heat. Once melted, add the sweetcorn and garlic. Fry for 5 minutes, stirring occasionally.

3   Meanwhile, put all of the ingredients for the jalapeño salsa into a blender and blitz to form a coarse salsa. (This can be made ahead and kept in the fridge for a few days.)

4   Stir the milk into the sweetcorn and bubble for another 5 minutes. Then, using a handheld blender or food processor, blend the mixture into a rough pulp, leaving some kernels whole. Pour into a medium-sized ovenproof dish and stir in the spring onions. Taste for seasoning, then top with the Cheddar.

5   Pop the dish into the hot oven and bake for around 15 minutes until golden and heated through. It should have a porridge-like consistency, and the cheese topping should be beginning to brown.

6   To serve, spoon the creamed corn into bowls, then top with the crispy red beans and drizzle with the jalapeño salsa.

Feeds 2 as a main, 4 as a side
Takes 40 minutes

1 shallot, roughly chopped

½ garlic bulb, sliced across the equator

2 bay leaves (fresh or dried)

5 thyme sprigs (optional)

1 tablespoon black peppercorns, toasted then crushed

1 tablespoon fennel seeds

1 dried chilli or a pinch of dried chilli flakes

4 fresh tarragon sprigs (or 1 teaspoon dried tarragon)

700g (1lb 9oz) jar Queen Butter Beans with their bean stock or 2 × 400g (14oz) cans butter beans, drained and rinsed with 200ml (7fl oz) veg stock

200ml (7fl oz) veg or chicken stock

60g (2¼oz) vegetarian hard cheese or Pecorino, grated (or Parmesan or a vegetarian alternative)

200g (7oz) asparagus, sliced lengthways (or grilled sliced courgettes, fried leeks or pan-fried sliced cabbage)

sea salt and freshly ground black pepper

For the herb topping

large bunch of herbs (about 30g/1oz), such as basil, parsley, mint, tarragon, or a mixture

juice of 1 lemon

30g (1oz) unsalted nuts, such as hazelnuts, almonds or pine nuts

1 small garlic clove

3 tablespoons olive oil

I've taken inspiration from one of my favourite pasta dishes, cacio e pepe. This is not a cacio e pepe in the traditional sense, but it shares the main ingredients – black pepper and Pecorino Romano cheese. By braising the beans in their own liquid, the sauce gets super creamy, just as it does when using starchy pasta water. You can vary the veg toppings endlessly for this dish, or just eat the beans and sauce as they are.

CACIO E PEPE BEANS

1 Take out a clean muslin bag or a piece of cheesecloth. Place the shallot, garlic, bay leaves, thyme, peppercorns, fennel seeds, chilli and tarragon inside, then tie it up.

2 Tip the beans and their bean or veg stock into a medium-sized saucepan. Pour over the veg or chicken stock and nestle in the little bag of spices. Let it all simmer on a low heat until reduced and quite thick and creamy. If you're using jarred beans, this will take about 20–30 minutes; if you're using canned beans, add 1 teaspoon salt and give them 40 minutes–1 hour, for a softer texture. Take care not to boil the beans, as they will go mushy.

3 Stir in the grated cheese and mix well. Season if needed.

4 Meanwhile, combine all the ingredients for the herb topping in a blender and blend. Alternatively, use a pestle and mortar. Season to taste.

5 With a few minutes of the beans' cooking time remaining, cook the asparagus in salted water for about 2 minutes, depending on the size.

6 To serve, scoop the beans into a shallow bowl or plate. Top with the asparagus, followed by dollops of the herby sauce.

Ali Slagle

For crispy breadcrumbs, blitz stale slices of your favourite bread in a food processor (or buy pre-made breadcrumbs like panko).

Whip out this hearty, veggie, one-pot dish as the autumnal season is approaching. It's one of those meals that is super-simple and has minimal ingredients, but offers guaranteed satisfaction and heartiness.

Feeds 3
Takes 40 minutes

FRENCH ONION WHITE BEAN BAKE

30g (1oz) salted butter

1 large white onion (white onions are sweeter, but brown onions will also work), thinly sliced

small handful of thyme sprigs, leaves picked

1 tablespoon apple cider vinegar or white wine vinegar

700g (1lb 9oz) jar white beans with their bean stock, or 2 × 400g (14oz) cans white beans, drained, with 200ml (7fl oz) veg or chicken stock

70g (2½oz) Gruyère, coarsely grated (or Comté, or a mix of 50g (1¾oz) mature Cheddar and 30g (1oz) Parmesan or Pecorino)

50g (1¾oz) crispy breadcrumbs mixed with 1 tablespoon olive oil, to top (optional)

sea salt and freshly ground black pepper

1 Preheat the oven to 200°C/180°C fan/400°F/gas mark 6.

2 Melt the butter in a medium-sized ovenproof saucepan or casserole dish over a medium–high heat. Add the onion and season with salt and pepper. Cover and cook for 5 minutes, stirring once or twice, until the onions are softened.

3 Remove the lid and add the thyme. Continue to cook for another 10–15 minutes. As they cook and browned bits appear, add a tablespoon or so of water and stir to combine. Once evaporated, add another tablespoon and repeat; this prevents the onions from burning and speeds the process up. You want them to be jammy and a deep golden brown. (If you can caramelise the onions for even longer, go for it: the darker their colour, the sweeter their flavour.)

4 Next, add the vinegar and stir until evaporated, then add the beans with their bean or veg or chicken stock. Season to taste and bring to the boil for a minute. If using canned beans, you may need to add more salt; bring to a simmer and cook for a further 6–8 minutes to allow the beans to soften.

5 Reduce the heat slightly, then sprinkle the cheese evenly over the top, followed by the breadcrumbs (if using), especially around the edges (this will give you delicious crispy bits).

6 Transfer to the oven and bake for roughly 8–10 minutes until the cheese has melted and browned in places. If the top is not as toasted as you'd like, bake for another minute or two. Serve and tuck in.

In this recipe, we smother a sweet and sticky Korean-inspired sauce over some crispy chickpeas to create some little umami bombs you won't be able to get enough of. If you're unfamiliar with gochujang, it's a Korean condiment that's oozing with sweet, salty and spicy flavours, and adds real depth to your food. The sesame and smashed cucumber salad adds a punch of acidity. We recommend serving this with some white rice.

Feeds 2 as a main with salad and rice
Takes 50 minutes

CRISPY GOCHUJANG CHICKPEAS

700g (1lb 9oz) jar chickpeas, or 2 × 400g (14oz) cans chickpeas, drained

3 tablespoons neutral oil

1 tablespoon gochujang paste

2 tablespoons soy sauce or tamari

1 tablespoon runny honey or maple syrup

2 garlic cloves, crushed

2 tablespoons grated ginger

sea salt and freshly ground black pepper

For the sesame cucumber salad

2 cucumbers (or radishes) sliced

1 large garlic clove, crushed

1 red chilli, finely sliced

1½ tablespoons rice vinegar or white wine vinegar

2 teaspoons soy sauce or tamari

1 tablespoon sesame seeds, toasted

1 tablespoon sesame oil

250g (9oz) cooked white rice, to serve

For the toppings (optional)

2 tablespoons sesame seeds, toasted

3–4 spring onions, sliced

nori seaweed, crumbled

1 Preheat the oven to 200°C/180°C fan/400°F/gas mark 6.

2 To make the cucumber salad, begin by trimming the ends of the cucumbers. Then, using a rolling pin, gently smash the cucumbers until they split (this creates a flavour you simply can't achieve from just cutting, and also allows them to better absorb the seasoning), then slice into small chunks and put into a sieve set over a bowl. Sprinkle with a good pinch of salt and toss to coat. Leave to sit to allow some of the cucumber water to release while you're cooking.

3 Rinse the chickpeas and pat them dry with paper towel, then tip into a baking dish. Toss with 2 tablespoons of the olive oil and season with salt and pepper. Roast for 25–30 minutes until crispy, tossing halfway through.

4 Meanwhile, tip the cucumber into a salad bowl, then add the rest of the salad ingredients. Toss to combine and set aside.

5 Combine the gochujang, soy sauce or tamari, honey or maple syrup, garlic and ginger in a medium-sized saucepan over a medium heat. Bring to a gentle simmer, stirring constantly. Cook for 2–3 minutes until fully combined and smelling fragrant.

6 Remove the chickpeas from the oven and stir into the saucepan. Continue to stir until the sauce reduces and thickens slightly; you want it to have a slightly sticky but glossy texture.

7 Remove from the heat and serve with the salad. We like serving this as a rice bowl, loading up each bowl first with rice, then cucumber salad and then chickpeas, before sprinkling over the optional toppings: sesame seeds, sliced spring onions and nori.

Everyone has had one of those days when you just crave hearty comfort food. This rich ragu, loaded with cheese, is made with many ingredients you may already have in the back of your cupboard. We like to make a batch of this ragu and keep it in the fridge all week to feast on. Bubble it up with some good-quality stock and turn it into a soup, or load it on to some sourdough toast. It's a friend that's best paired with a glass of red wine. We love the contrasting flavours and textures when serving it with a fresh, creamy cheese.

RED BEAN RAGU WITH RICOTTA + PARMESAN

Feeds 6
Takes 1 hour

5 tablespoons olive oil, plus extra to serve

2 carrots, finely diced

1 celery stalk, finely diced

500g (1lb 2oz) mushrooms, finely chopped

2 bay leaves (fresh or dried) (optional)

2 small onions or 3 banana shallots, finely chopped

2 garlic cloves, crushed

1 teaspoon dried mixed herbs or oregano (or freshly chopped herbs: rosemary, thyme and parsley)

½ teaspoon dried chilli flakes

300ml (10fl oz) red wine or red vermouth

700g (1lb 9oz) jar red beans with their bean stock, or 2 x 400g (14oz) cans red kidney beans, drained, with 200ml (7fl oz) veg stock

400g (14oz) can chopped tomatoes

1 chicken or veggie stock cube

250g (9oz) ricotta (or torn mozzarella, goat's curd, burrata or queso fresco)

1 Heat the oil in a large, deep saucepan over a medium heat. Add the carrots, celery, mushrooms, bay leaves and onions, along with ½ teaspoon salt. Give the mixture a good stir so that the veggies are coated, then sweat for 15–20 minutes, stirring occasionally, until the ingredients are beginning to soften and have shrunk significantly. It may seem like a lot of oil, but when creating a meat-free ragu, you need to bring in the fat from elsewhere, so don't be afraid of this!

2 Add the garlic, herbs, and chilli flakes. Increase the heat to medium–high and cook for 1 minute. If there is still some liquid in the pan from the mushrooms, cook for a little longer until this is reduced and some of the base begins to stick to the bottom of the pan.

3 Pour in the red wine or vermouth, deglazing any veg that had begun to caramelise at the bottom of the pan. Allow the alcohol to cook off for 5–8 minutes, then reduce the heat to low simmer and add the red beans with their bean or veg stock, breaking them up in your hands as you go to allow some to thicken the sauce. If using unsalted canned beans, make sure to add a good pinch of salt here.

4 Tip in the chopped tomatoes and mix through. At this point, add the stock cube, breaking it up with your fingers and letting it dissolve in the liquid of the stew. Bubble for 20 minutes for jarred beans, or 26–28 minutes for canned, adding a splash of water if it becomes too dry.

5 While you're waiting for the ragu to thicken, spoon the ricotta into a bowl. Lightly mash using a fork, and season with a pinch of salt.

500g (1lb 2oz) long pasta

100g (3½oz) Parmesan (or Pecorino, Grana Padano or veggie alternative) grated

small bunch of basil (about 15g/½oz), optional

sea salt and freshly ground black pepper

6 Cook the pasta according to the packet instructions (but make sure your water is salty!). Once cooked, drain, then drizzle with some olive oil. Using tongs, tumble the pasta on to 6 plates. Spoon over the ragu and dollop the ricotta on top. Finish with a generous grating of Parmesan and torn basil leaves (if using).

Feeds 4
Takes 20 minutes

2 tablespoons extra virgin olive oil, plus extra to serve

1 onion (red or white) or 2 banana shallots, very finely chopped

1 large carrot, finely chopped

2 celery stalks, finely chopped

2 fat garlic cloves, crushed

small pinch of dried chilli flakes

2 rosemary or thyme sprigs, leaves finely chopped

2 teaspoons tomato purée

400g (14oz) passata (or chopped tomatoes, blitzed until smooth)

1 teaspoon white caster sugar

1 litre (1¾ pints) chicken or veg stock (fresh is best if you can get it), plus extra if needed

1 vegetarian hard cheese (or Parmesan) rind

1 fresh bay leaf (optional)

700g (1lb 9oz) jar white beans with their bean stock, or 2 × 400g (14oz) cans white beans with 200ml (7fl oz) chicken or veg stock

100g (3½oz) dried lasagne sheets, broken up into bite-sized pieces (or any other pasta)

200g (7oz) cavolo nero (or regular kale or cabbage) thickly sliced

sea salt and freshly ground black pepper

vegetarian hard cheese or Parmesan, grated

sourdough or foccacia, to serve

Since before anyone can remember, the people of Tuscany have been nicknamed 'Mangiafagioli', or 'Bean-eaters'. This rich and satisfying classic bean soup can be remixed with whatever pasta shapes (or beans, for that matter) you have in your cupboard. Serve it on a cold winter's day for proper comfort food. It's a great way to use up those three random pasta sheets you have left over after making a lasagne.

PASTA E FAGIOLI

1   Heat the oil in a lidded saucepan or casserole dish over a low heat. Add the onion, carrot and celery, along with a pinch of salt, and fry for 10–12 minutes, or until softened and translucent.

2   Add the garlic, chilli and rosemary or thyme, and fry for another 2 minutes. Stir through the tomato purée and cook for a further minute, before adding the passata, sugar, stock, Parmesan rind and bay leaf, if using. Stir, then tip in the beans, along with their bean or veg stock. If using canned beans, add an extra pinch of salt at this point. Cook, covered, for 20 minutes over a low–medium heat, stirring often.

3   After 20 minutes, throw in the pasta and simmer for a further 5 minutes, then add the cavolo nero. Top up with more stock if it's looking too thick. The soup is ready when the pasta is cooked.

4   Top with a good drizzle of extra virgin olive oil and the grated cheese, and serve with a hunk of sourdough or focaccia.

Smoky, spicy and a little bit nutty, this ragu hits all the right spots. The burnt aubergine technique creates a soft and fleshy aubergine centre which melts into the sauce of the chickpeas. The richness of the tomatoes and harissa works wonders, topped with the charred broccoli for freshness and crunch. Try dolloping over some Greek yogurt too, if you like. Serve with couscous or orzo if you want a heartier affair.

Feeds 2–3
Takes 30 minutes

SMOKY HARISSA AUBERGINE + CHICKPEAS

1 large aubergine

1 tablespoon olive oil

2 large garlic cloves, grated

1 tablespoon tomato purée

2 teaspoons smoked paprika

1 heaped tablespoon harissa paste

700g (1lb 9oz) jar Queen Chickpeas or 1 Chickpea Base (page 184), with their bean stock

sea salt and freshly ground black pepper

lemon wedges, to serve

For the charred broccoli crunch

200g (7oz) long-stem or purple sprouting broccoli, trimmed (or regular broccoli, cut into florets)

1 tablespoon olive oil

2 tablespoons mixed seeds

To serve (optional)

orzo or couscous, Greek or natural yogurt or plant-based alternative

If you prefer your broccoli a little softer, blanch it in boiling water for 2 minutes before grilling.

1 Preheat the grill to high and place the aubergine directly under the hot grill. Cook, turning regularly, for 10 minutes until totally blackened and collapsing – it should feel soft and squidgy. Transfer to a bowl and cover with clingfilm (leave the grill on). Leave to steam while you make the broccoli.

2 To make the charred broccoli, tip the broccoli on to a roasting tray. Drizzle with the olive oil and season with salt and pepper, then toss well to coat. Grill for 8–10 minutes until nicely charred. For the last 30 seconds, add the mixed seeds to toast.

3 Once the aubergine is cool enough to handle, peel away the skin and shred the flesh using a fork. It should be soft and slightly mushy, and the skin should pull away easily. Discard the skin and mash the flesh with a fork.

4 Heat the oil in a large saucepan over a medium heat. Add the garlic and cook for 1 minute until fragrant, then stir in the tomato purée and let it fry off for 2–3 minutes. Add the smoked paprika and harissa paste and stir to combine.

5 Add the aubergine flesh and stir, evenly coating it in all of the spices. Reserve 2–3 tablespoons of the bean stock and drain the rest. Add the chickpeas to the pan with the reserved bean stock and season with salt and pepper, to taste. Add more liquid if you feel it's necessary.

6 Plate up the chickpeas and top with the charred broccoli and seeds. Serve with lemon wedges, for squeezing, and any other chosen accompaniments.

My version of rajma chawal or 'red beans and rice' is served like a Buddha bowl to ramp up the flavours and textures. It's a frugal recipe that can be batch-cooked, taken to work the next day or made for the whole family as a low-fat, protein-rich one-pot wonder. Serve with a kachumber salad (see opposite) and yogurt of your choice. A few cheeky poppadoms also delight!

Feeds 4
Takes 55 minutes

RAJMA MASALA BUDDHA BOWL

1 tablespoon neutral oil

1 teaspoon cumin seeds

4 cardamom pods

4 cloves

1 cinnamon stick

1 bay leaf (fresh or dried)

2 onions, very finely diced

1 tablespoon ginger and garlic paste

1 green chilli, finely diced

1 teaspoon tomato purée

1 teaspoon each ground coriander, ground cumin and ground red Kashmiri chilli

½ teaspoon ground turmeric

200ml (7fl oz) passata or blitzed canned tomatoes

700g (1lb 9oz) jar red beans with their bean stock, or 2 × 400g (14oz) cans red kidney beans, drained, with 200ml (7fl oz) veg stock

1 tablespoon kasuri methi (optional)

1 teaspoon garam masala

white caster sugar, to taste

small handful chopped fresh coriander

1 tablespoon ghee, butter or coconut oil

sea salt and freshly ground black pepper

1 Heat the oil over a medium heat. Add all the whole spices and bay leaf and sizzle for 30 seconds, then tip in the finely diced onion. Spend about 10 minutes slowly browning the onion until it's a deep caramel colour.

2 Add the garlic and ginger paste, along with the green chilli. Stir-fry for about 30 seconds. Adding the ingredients in this fashion will give you a richer-tasting result. Add the tomato purée and all the ground spices (other than the garam masala). Reduce the heat to low and stir to combine, then tip in the passata. Leave to simmer for about 10 minutes until you see the oil rising to the surface.

3 Now add the red beans with their bean or veg stock. Add the kasuri methi (if using) and garam masala, then cover and simmer for 5 minutes. Remove the lid and simmer for another 5 minutes, ensuring the beans are not sticking to the bottom of the pan. If using canned beans, simmer for a little longer for that softer texture, and season with extra salt. Once the sauce is a rich, deep colour, mash a few of the beans with a fork to give the soupy curry some thickness if needed. Taste for seasoning and adjust with salt and sugar as required.

4 Stir through the ghee, butter or coconut oil to finish, and top with a flurry of fresh coriander.

5 To serve as a Buddha bowl, I suggest you take a wide bowl and add a generous helping of rice, followed by some rajma masala. Top with yogurt swirled with pickle or chutney, and serve with poppadoms and kachumber salad. If you've made the garam masala sweet potatoes, too, they will add another texture and some sweetness to the bowl. Enjoy!

To serve

basmati rice

poppadoms

kachumber salad

garam masala sweet potatoes

Kachumber Salad

Slice half a cucumber into half-moons, roughly grate 1 carrot, slice 4 radishes, quarter 8 baby tomatoes, thinly slice half a red onion and cube 1 avocado. Toss everything together in a mixing bowl with a pinch of sea salt and mint sauce, or just a good squeeze of lemon.

Garam Masala Sweet Potatoes

Chop one large sweet potato into small cubes (no need to peel). Toss with 1 tsp of garam masala, 1 tbsp of olive oil and a pinch of salt, then roast for 40 minutes at 200°C/180°C fan/400°F/gas mark 6.

Japanese cooking rarely involves beans within the haricot family, but the combination of umami-rich miso paste with creamy, soft white beans is a thing of magic. It also lends itself to so many variations, which feel different each time. All that's required is texture (crunch, bite) and acidity (through a pickle or otherwise). We like loading the warm miso beans into bowls and topping them with kimchi, cooked green veggies and chilli oil, but you could also serve up a more refined dish, using the beans as a side to slow-cooked aubergine or pork and a crunchy cucumber salad (see page 60).

Feeds 2
Takes 10 minutes

MISO BEANS

25g (1oz) butter or plant-based alternative

1 shallot (or 4 spring onions (use the white parts for the base and the green parts as a topping) or 1 small white onion), finely diced

1 garlic clove, finely sliced

700g (1lb 9oz) jar white beans, or 1 White Bean Base (page 184), with their bean stock

juice of ½ lemon (or ½ tablespoon rice vinegar)

2 teaspoons miso (we used brown miso, but use whatever you have!)

Suggested toppings

handful of cooked broccoli, or any other green vegetable

handful of grated carrot

1 tablespoon kimchi, pickled radishes or pickled cucumbers

Soft-boiled egg, shredded cooked chicken or pork, or fried tofu

freshly chopped coriander or chives

chilli oil, to taste

handful of chopped roasted cashews, peanuts or sesame seeds

1 Melt the butter in a medium-sized saucepan over a low heat. Add the shallot and cook for a few minutes, then add the garlic. Once translucent, add the beans, along with all of their bean stock.

2 Let the beans bubble away for a few minutes, mashing them up as you go to reach your desired consistency. Add the lemon juice and miso paste and stir to combine. Keep cooking for a couple of minutes, adding a splash of water if the mixture looks too thick, just to make sure the miso has melted through the beans.

3 Pour your miso beans into a bowl and top with whatever you fancy.

Vegan Option

Make this dish vegan by simply omiting the egg.

HEARTY SALADS 5

When winter approaches, there are only so many soups and stews we can consume before we feel like curling up on the sofa, with no intention of moving until Christmas. For those times when you're craving something a little lighter, but still with some indulgence, this festive salad number will do the trick. Get your hands on the ripest of pears, if you can, then team them up with a creamy, tangy blue cheese, crunchy walnuts and radicchio or chicory for a hint of bitterness. Try a little drizzle of honey over the top if you're feeling sweet.

Feeds 4
Takes 20–25 minutes

PEAR, BLUE CHEESE + WALNUT SALAD

2 heads of radicchio, or 250g (9oz) red chicory

juice of 1 lemon

2–3 tablespoons extra virgin olive oil, plus extra to serve (optional)

large bunch of parsley (about 30g/1oz), finely chopped

small bunch of chives (about 15g/½oz), finely chopped (or dill)

700g (1lb 9oz) jar Queen Butter Beans, or 1 Butter Bean Base (page 184), drained

3 pears, thinly sliced

100g (3½oz) Roquefort or gorgonzola, torn into medium-sized chunks

small handful of walnuts, toasted, some left whole, some chopped

sea salt

1 Remove any tatty outer leaves from the radicchio. Trim the core and roughly tear the leaves apart, chopping any larger ones.

2 Add the leaves to a large mixing bowl, along with the lemon juice, olive oil and a pinch of salt. Add the parsley and chives and stir to combine.

3 Next, add the beans, pears and cheese and carefully fold into the rest of the salad, trying not to break up the cheese too much.

4 Divide the salad between 4 plates and sprinkle over the walnuts. Finish with a squeeze of lemon and an extra drizzle of olive oil, if you like.

This warm winter salad is a textural sensation. The balsamic reduces around the puffy red beans and contrasts beautifully with the mildly bitter kale. Cheesy things make a killer combo with this dish, so either include the shaved Parmesan or make it more of a feast by serving it alongside a rich cauliflower cheese or an old-school mac and cheese.

STICKY BALSAMIC KALE + RED BEAN WINTER SALAD

Feeds 3
Takes 25 minutes

2 tablespoons rapeseed oil

700g (1lb 9oz) jar red beans or 1 Red Bean Base (page 184), drained

4 tablespoons good-quality balsamic reduction or glaze

1 tablespoon demerara or soft light brown sugar, if needed

200g (7oz) kale or cavolo nero, roughly chopped

sea salt and freshly ground black pepper

shavings of Parmesan cheese or veggie alternative, to serve (optional)

1 Preheat the oven to 220°C/200°C fan/425°F/gas mark 7.

2 Add 1 tablespoon of the rapeseed oil to a large roasting tin and put into the oven to heat up for 2–3 minutes.

3 Add the red beans, along with 2 tablespoons of the balsamic vinegar and a good grinding of black pepper. Give the beans a mix so that they are fully coated.

4 Taste a little of your balsamic vinegar on the tip of your finger. If it's very sweet, don't add the demerara; if it's acidic, sprinkle the sugar over the beans.

5 Transfer the tray to the oven and roast for 10–15 minutes until the beans are starting to turn crisp.

6 Remove from the oven and add the kale to the roasting tray, along with the remaining 2 tablespoons balsamic vinegar and 1 tablespoon of oil. Sprinkle with salt and toss to combine.

7 Return the tray to the oven and roast for a further 5 minutes until the kale is crisp and a little charred.

8 Serve immediately, topped with the Parmesan shavings, if using.

Crisp and golden butter beans, sweet jammy figs, sharp and salty Pecorino and a zingy, creamy pistachio dressing – this little salad ticks all the boxes. Perfect during late summer/early autumn when figs are at their best. I love adding beans to so many things, salads especially, to instantly bulk them up and add some substance.

ROAST FIG, BUTTER BEAN + PECORINO SALAD

Feeds 2
Takes 35–40 minutes

100g (3½oz) shelled pistachios

½ 700g (1lb 9oz) jar butter beans, or ½ Butter Bean Base (page 184), drained

3 large, ripe figs, quartered

1 tablespoon olive oil

small bunch of thyme (about 15g/½oz), leaves picked

25g (1oz) aged Pecorino, Parmesan or veggie alternative, shaved

sea salt

lamb's lettuce or rocket, to serve

For the dressing

5 tbsp extra virgin olive oil, plus extra to serve

20ml (¾fl oz) white wine vinegar or apple cider vinegar

½ garlic clove, crushed

1 teaspoon honey

juice of 1 lemon

10g (¼oz) aged Pecorino, Parmesan or veggie alternative

1   Preheat the oven to 180°C/160°C fan/350°F/gas mark 4 and line a baking tray with foil.

2   Tip the pistachios on to a separate baking tray and roast for around 12–15 minutes, until toasted and fragrant. Leave to cool, and increase the oven temperature to 220°C/200°C fan/425°F/gas mark 7.

3   Rinse the drained beans and pat them dry with a paper towel. Tip into a bowl, then add the figs, olive oil, thyme and a pinch of salt. Toss well and transfer to the prepared baking tray. Spread out evenly so that the ingredients aren't piled on top of each other, then roast for 20–25 minutes, until the figs are jammy and the beans are crisp.

4   To make the dressing, transfer 60g (2¼oz) of the cooled pistachios to a small blender, along with all the dressing ingredients. Add a pinch of salt and blitz to emulsify. You may need to loosen with a tablespoon or two of cold water to reach a drizzly consistency. It should look like a runny pesto. Taste for seasoning, adding more salt if needed. Set aside.

5   When everything's ready, assemble the salad. Toss a few good handfuls of lamb's lettuce or rocket with some extra virgin olive oil and season with salt. Divide between 3 plates and top with the figs and beans, drizzling over any juice from the pan. Scatter over the Pecorino or Parmesan shavings, then drizzle with the dressing. Finish by roughly chopping the remaining pistachios and scattering on top. Serve immediately.

 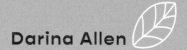

I love this perky Mexican salad, and make it throughout the year with either fresh or canned sweetcorn. The limey dressing packs a punch, while the sweetness of the corn and peppers cuts through the zestiness. I've had a love affair with Mexico for several decades. The flavour of this vibrant, colourful bean salad transports me back to the Abastos Market in Oaxaca – it's Mexico on a plate.

OAXACAN-STYLE BLACK BEAN SALAD

Feeds 6
Takes 15 minutes

700g (1lb 9oz) jar black beans or 2 × 400g (14oz) cans black beans, drained

200g (7oz) can sweetcorn, drained

2 red peppers, diced

2 garlic cloves, crushed or grated

2 shallots or 1 banana shallot, finely chopped

¼ teaspoon cayenne pepper or hot chilli powder

large bunch of coriander (about 30g/1oz), chopped

2 ripe but firm avocados (preferably Hass), diced

sea salt and freshly ground black pepper

corn tortilla chips, to serve

For the dressing

9 tablespoons extra virgin olive oil

1 teaspoon lime zest

6 tablespoons freshly squeezed lime juice

1–2 tablespoons white caster sugar

1 Put the black beans, sweetcorn, red peppers, garlic and shallot into a bowl. Sprinkle over the cayenne and most of the chopped coriander and season to taste. Toss gently to combine.

2 To make the dressing, mix together the extra virgin olive oil and lime zest and juice in a small bowl. Add 1 tablespoon of the sugar and whisk to combine. Season to taste and add a little more sugar if necessary to balance the lime. Pour over the salad and toss.

3 Just before serving, add the avocados and mix gently.

4 Garnish with the remaining coriander and serve at room temperature, with lots of tortilla chips on the side.

Heavy on the herbs, this zippy salad needs to be eaten IMMEDIATELY. If you dress the herbs and radishes and then let them sit, you'll lose both fragrance and crunch – essential components to this dish. Marinating the beans with balsamic, plump dried fruit and salty capers gives this salad a real punch. Serve it in early summer; we like it alongside some Muhammara Chickpeas (page 24).

Feeds 4
Takes 20 minutes

RADISHING BEAN + HERB SALAD

700g (1lb 9oz) jar red beans, or 1 Red Bean Base (page 184), drained

500g (1lb 2oz) radishes (the more colourful, the more drama), sliced as thinly as possible (use a mandoline if you have one)

small bunch of flat-leaf parsley (about 15g/½oz), roughly chopped

small bunch of mint (about 10g/¼oz), leaves roughly chopped

small bunch of dill (about 15g/½oz), roughly chopped

small bunch of chives (about 15g/½oz) chives, chopped into 2.5cm (1in) pieces (optional)

150g (5½oz) walnuts, toasted and roughly chopped (or almonds)

150g (5½oz) feta or vegan alternative, crumbled

sea salt and freshly ground black pepper

For the dressing

1½ tablespoons balsamic vinegar

1 tablespoon lemon juice

30g (1oz) raisins or sultanas

½ garlic clove, roughly chopped

1 tablespoon capers

4 tablespoons extra virgin olive oil

1 To make the dressing, add all of the dressing ingredients to a bowl and whisk to combine. Add the drained beans, season to taste, and leave to marinate briefly while you prepare the rest of the salad.

2 Put the radishes into a salad bowl and season with a pinch of salt. Spoon out the red beans from the dressing and toss to combine, reserving the bulk of the marinade to drizzle over at the end.

3 In a medium-sized bowl, combine the chopped herbs, walnuts and feta, tossing gently so that you don't break up the cheese too much.

4 Sprinkle this mixture over the salad and serve immediately, drizzled with the remaining marinade.

WARNING: this salad is not for the meek and mild. It's citrusy, salty and bold, but we adore it – rein in the lemon if you prefer things more gently done. The trick is to dress the fennel at the very last minute, so that it retains its crispness; this is a crucial element to the salad. You can use any bean here, but we love the black bean, which contrasts beautifully with the fresh and bright green coming from the rest of the ingredients. Serve this with full-fat Greek yogurt, steak or a juicy pork chop.

Feeds 2
Takes 10 minutes

FURIOUS FENNEL + BLACK BEAN SALAD

large handful of green olives (in oil), pitted and chopped

2 small fennel bulbs or 1 large, thinly sliced (use a mandoline, if you have one)

½ 700g (1lb 9oz) jar black beans, or ½ Black Bean Base (page 184), drained

80–100g (2¾–3½oz) shelled pistachios, toasted and roughly chopped (we like bigger chunks for the crunch factor)

small bunch of mint (about 15g/½oz), leaves picked and torn if large

½ teaspoon dried chilli flakes

100ml (3½fl oz) extra virgin olive oil

juice of 1 lemon

50g (1¾oz) vegetarian hard cheese or Parmesan, shaved

sea salt and freshly ground black pepper

thick Greek yogurt, to serve

1 Add the olives, fennel, black beans, pistachios, mint and chilli flakes to a large mixing bowl. Add the olive oil and lemon juice, along with a good pinch of salt and pepper. Toss well to coat.

2 Divide between 2 plates and scatter over the Parmesan shavings. Serve immediately, with a dollop of Greek yogurt on the side.

A nod to the old-school classic, this version makes the dressing the base for some epic toppings: garlic, chilli, honey-glazed halloumi and savoury white beans, with the grilled lettuce wedges as the centrepiece. In many ways, it's not really a salad at all, but a killer veggie main. Serve this alone, or with some fresh toast to mop up any dressing that remains.

Feeds 4
Takes 20 minutes

GREEN GODDESS SALAD

2 tablespoons olive oil

2 romaine or Cos lettuces, sliced in half with the stalks intact

700g (1lb 9oz) jar white beans, or 1 White Bean Base (page 184), drained

100g (3½oz) edamame beans (see Tip)

sea salt and freshly ground black pepper

For the honey-glazed halloumi

225g (8oz) halloumi, cut into 2cm (¾in) cubes

2 tablespoons runny honey

1 teaspoon dried chilli flakes

juice of ½ lemon

For the green goddess dressing

50g (1¾oz) mixed fresh herbs: tarragon, dill, parsley and mint

1 tablespoon capers

juice of 1 lemon

150g (5½oz) Greek yogurt

2 tablespoons olive oil

1 shallot, roughly chopped

1 tablespoon mayonnaise (optional)

1 garlic clove, crushed

½–1 teaspoon Dijon or English mustard

1 First, put your halloumi in a shallow bowl and slather the cubes in the honey, chilli flakes and lemon juice. Put in the fridge to marinate for 15 minutes.

2 To make the dressing, put all the ingredients into a food processor and blend until smooth. Season to taste.

3 Heat 1 tablespoon of the oil in a wide frying pan over a high heat. Add the lettuce 'wedges' cut-side down, and fry for 2 minutes until they're a little browned. You're looking to char the underside without cooking the lettuce. Set aside.

4 Reduce the heat to medium–high and, using the same pan, heat the remaining oil. Add the marinated halloumi cubes, ensuring they don't stick together. Fry the halloumi for 2–3 minutes on each side, checking regularly to see that it doesn't burn.

5 To serve, pour half of the dressing on to a large serving platter. Top with the lettuce wedges, then dress the surrounding area with the white beans. Scatter over the edamame and top with the glazed halloumi. Serve immediately, with the rest of the dressing on the side. You can use any left over for another cracking salad as it keeps for 3–5 days.

Feel free to use frozen edamame here: simply defrost in a little boiling water, then run under cold water to cool.

CLASSICS REIMAGINED

These salads are quick assembly jobs. Once everything is prepped, you can simply toss the ingredients together, drizzle over the dressing and you're good to go.

Here, the chickpeas replace the chicken, but you could have a go at including the chicken and using the chickpeas as gluten-free croutons instead. Both work. For extra pizzazz, we've given options to crisp up the beans for added texture but if you're short of time, just toss them in as they are.

Feeds 4
Takes 10–15 minutes

CHICKPEA CAESAR SALAD

700g (1lb 9oz) jar chickpeas or 2 × 400g (14oz) cans chickpeas, drained

small loaf of crusty bread, roughly torn into 2.5cm (1in) pieces

1½ tablespoons olive oil

1 teaspoon paprika

100g (3½oz) kale leaves, stems removed

large head of Cos or romaine lettuce, leaves separated and torn into bite-sized pieces

50g (1¾oz) Parmesan or veggie alternative, grated or shaved

sea salt and freshly ground black pepper

For the dressing

1 garlic clove, crushed

4 tablespoons olive oil

juice of 1 lemon

6 anchovy fillets, from a tin or jar (optional)

2 teaspoons Dijon mustard

4 tablespoons mayonnaise

1 Preheat the oven to 200°C/180°C fan/400°F/gas mark 6.

2 Rinse the chickpeas and pat dry with a paper towel. Scatter them over a baking tray, then add the bread chunks. Drizzle with 1 tablespoonof the olive oil and sprinkle with paprika and a pinch of salt (more than a pinch if using unsalted canned beans!). Bake for 8–10 minutes, turning a few times so that everything browns evenly.

3 To make the dressing, add all the dressing ingredients to a food processor and blend well to combine. You're looking for the consistency of yogurt, so if it's a little too thick, add a few splashes of water to loosen. Season with freshly ground black pepper.

4 In a large bowl, combine the kale and remaining ½ tablespoon olive oil. Using your hands, massage the kale until slightly softened. Add the lettuce leaves.

5 Scatter over the chickpeas, croutons and half of the dressing, and toss well to combine.

6 Scatter over the Parmesan and drizzle over the remaining dressing. Serve immediately.

Here, beans bring some nuttiness to an absolute classic:
tuna Niçoise.

Feeds 4
Takes 30 minutes

CHICKPEA + TUNA NIÇOISE

250g (9oz) green beans, trimmed

4 eggs

200g (7oz) radishes, thinly sliced

15g (½oz) chives, chopped (or parsley)

4 spring onions, thinly sliced

150g (5½oz) mixed salad leaves – try to go for a mix of textures, such as watercress and Little Gem lettuce

700g (1lb 9oz) jar chickpeas or 1 Chickpea Base (page 184), drained and rinsed

2 tablespoons capers

large handful of Kalamata olives (around 30g/1oz), pitted (or olives of your choice)

50g (1¾oz) sun-dried tomatoes in oil, finely chopped

2 x 200g (7oz) cans tuna in olive oil, drained

sea salt and freshly ground black pepper

For the dressing

1 tablespoon Dijon mustard

juice of 1 lemon

1 teaspoon honey

3–4 tablespoons extra virgin olive oil

1 To make the dressing, whisk together all of the dressing ingredients in a bowl. Add a splash of water to loosen, if necessary, and a pinch of salt, to taste. Set aside in the fridge until ready to serve.

2 Bring a large pan of lightly salted water to the boil and blanch the green beans for roughly 2 minutes until tender. Scoop out into a colander, and rinse under cold running water until completely cold, then set aside.

3 With the pan of boiling water still on the heat, gently lower in the eggs and simmer for 6–7 minutes, depending on their size, then drain and run under cold water until cold. Peel and slice each one in half.

4 Add the green beans, sliced radishes, chives, spring onions and salad leaves to a large salad bowl and mix together. Toss in the chickpeas, along with the capers, olives, sun-dried tomatoes and tuna. Arrange the eggs on top, and drizzle over the dressing to serve.

Try this with the Chilli Crispy Chickpeas on page 75, for a crunchy alternative

Beck Johnson

Feeds 2–3
Takes 15 minutes

1 red onion, finely diced

juice of 2 limes, plus lime wedges to serve

1 garlic clove, crushed

700g (1lb 9oz) jar chickpeas or 1 Chickpea Base (page 184), drained

½ cucumber, chopped

150g (5½oz) cherry tomatoes, quartered

100g (3½oz) sugar snap peas, sliced into thirds

large bunch of coriander (about 30g/1oz), finely chopped

dried chilli flakes (optional)

sea salt

For the dressing

4 tablespoons crunchy peanut butter

2 tablespoons rice wine vinegar or white wine vinegar

3 tablespoons soy sauce or tamari

2 tablespoons sesame oil

1 teaspoon white or brown miso

1 tablespoon maple syrup or honey

1 teaspoon ground turmeric

1 tablespoon hot sauce (optional)

To serve

8 Little Gem lettuce leaves

100g (3½oz) cooked white rice

shop-bought crispy onions (optional)

2 tablespoons sesame seeds

salted peanuts, crushed

1–2 mild red chillies, sliced

This one's for the peanut butter-lovers. These chickpeas are dressed in a glossy, satay-style sauce, which we love to nestle into crunchy lettuce boats. The zesty limes cut through the richness, and the crispy fried onions top everything off with the perfect crunch. If you feel like something a little heartier, serve the chickpeas as part of a rice bowl .

CHICKPEA SATAY BOATS

1 In a small bowl, combine the red onion, lime juice and garlic with a pinch of sea salt. Stir and set aside.

2 In a separate medium-sized bowl, combine all of the dressing ingredients and mix well.

3 Add the chickpeas to the bowl with the dressing and stir until they are fully coated in the sauce. Then add the cucumber, tomatoes, sugar snap peas and coriander, followed by the onion and lime juice mix. Toss well. Add chilli flakes at this point if you like a bit of a kick.

4 To serve, use the lettuce leaves as 'boats' for the filling. If using cooked rice, sprinkle some into each lettuce boat, then top with the satay chickpeas, followed by some crispy onions (if using) and sesame seeds. Sprinkle over the crushed peanuts for some added crunch, and garnish with the sliced fresh chilli. Finish with another squeeze of lime if you like it zesty.

Beth Adamson

> If you want to save on time and energy, skip frying the cauliflower steaks and roast with the chickpeas, broken into florets – but don't overload the tray or they won't crisp up.

Feeds 2 as a main, 4 as a side
Takes 30 minutes

½ 700g (1lb 9oz) jar chickpeas or 400g (14oz) can chickpeas, drained

3 tablespoons olive oil, plus extra to serve

1 teaspoon smoked paprika or chilli powder (optional, if you'd like some heat)

1 small cauliflower, sliced into 'steaks' about 1cm (½in) thick (or broccoli)

70g (2½oz) feta (or grilled halloumi)

small bunch of dill or parsley (about 15g/½oz), finely chopped

sea salt and freshly ground black pepper

For the creamy tahini base

1 tablespoon tahini

3 tablespoons Greek yogurt or crème fraîche

juice of 1 lemon

For the quick pickled onion

1 red onion, finely sliced

1 teaspoon runny honey or maple syrup

juice of 1 lime

I love roasted chickpeas. I tumble them on to toast, toss with shaved asparagus in a salad and load them on to dips. But this combination of caramelised cauliflower, tangy feta and creamy tahini dressing is the one I come back to time and time again. Serve alone or have as part of a mezze feast with koftas or falafel.

CARAMELISED CAULIFLOWER CHICKPEAS

1 Preheat the oven to 200°C/180°C fan/400°F/gas mark 6.

2 Rinse the chickpeas, then tumble them on to a baking tray and pat dry with a paper towel. Drizzle with 2 tabelspoons of the olive oil, then season with the paprika or chilli powder, if using, black pepper and a pinch of salt (add more than a pinch if using unsalted canned chickpeas). Roast for 25 minutes until golden and crispy, shaking the chickpeas halfway through to prevent sticking.

3 Meanwhile, heat the remaining 1 tablespoon oil in a frying pan over a medium heat. Add the cauliflower 'steaks' and cook for about 5 minutes until golden, then flip and colour on the other side for a further 5 minutes. Do this in batches until all of the 'steaks' are cooked.

4 To make the creamy tahini base, mix together the tahini, yogurt and lemon juice in a bowl until you have a creamy consistency. Add a dash of water to loosen, if necessary. Season to taste and refrigerate until ready to serve.

5 For the quick pickled onions, combine all the ingredients in a small bowl and season well with salt. Scrunch the onion into the lime juice and honey mixture, and set aside to quickly pickle.

6 When everything is ready, spoon the tahini mixture on to your serving plate and spread with the back of a spoon. Place the cauliflower steaks on top, then sprinkle over the crispy chickpeas and crumble over the feta. Drizzle with some extra olive oil, and top with the chopped herbs and the pickled onions.

On a hot summer's day, there is little more to crave than a juicy watermelon and feta salad. Adding the black beans turns this into a dish that is hearty and light all at once. If you're feeling lazy, don't make the pangrattato, but make sure you add the Kalamata olives; their mellow, bitter flavour brings the dish firmly into the savoury camp. We like serving this with warm pittas, dressed in a drizzle of good olive oil.

Feeds 2
Takes 10–15 minutes

BLACK BEAN, WATERMELON + FETA SALAD

1 small red onion, halved and thinly sliced

juice of 2 large lemons (use the zest in the pangrattato below)

½ 700g (1lb 9oz) jar black beans, or ½ Black Bean Base (page 1840), drained

2 tablespoons extra virgin olive oil

1.5kg (3lb 5oz) sweet, ripe watermelon (roughly 1 small watermelon), rind and pips removed, flesh chopped into walnut-sized pieces

200g (7oz) feta, chopped into 2cm (¾in) cubes

small bunch of mint (about 15g/½oz), leaves picked

sea salt and freshly ground black pepper

For the pangrattato

2 tablespoons extra virgin olive oil

100g (3½oz) coarse breadcrumbs of choice (dried or fresh are fine)

1 garlic clove, crushed

100g (3½oz) Kalamata olives, pitted and finely chopped

zest of 2 large lemons

1 teaspoon dried chilli flakes (optional)

1 In a small bowl, combine the red onion with the lemon juice and leave to soak; this gets rid of the onion's pungency but helps retain the bite.

2 To make the pangrattato, heat the olive oil in a heavy-based frying pan over a medium heat. Add the breadcrumbs and stir for 2–3 minutes, or until lightly toasted. Add the garlic and stir to combine, then remove from the heat. Stir in the olives, lemon zest and chilli flakes (if using), then season to taste.

3 Spread out the beans on a large serving plate or in a large shallow bowl. Drizzle with the olive oil, then give the beans a stir. Top with the watermelon and feta, then sprinkle over the mint. Scatter the onions over the salad, then drizzle over their juices.

4 Finish with the pangrattato and serve immediately.

BIG BEANS BEST

Using raw courgette ribbons makes this salad the freshest of the three, tossed through a light and zesty dressing and tang from the Parmesan. This salad is fairly stripped back on ingredients, so we recommend sourcing big beans for this recipe to really make each component sing.

Feeds 2
Takes 15–20 minutes

RAW COURGETTE RIBBON SALAD

3 courgettes (we like a mix of yellow and green, if you can get them)

zest and juice of 1 lemon

½–1 garlic clove, crushed (depending on how much of a garlic fan you are)

3 tablespoons olive oil

1 tablespoon balsamic vinegar or good-quality sherry/red wine vinegar

700g (1lb 9oz) jar Queen Butter Beans, or 1 White Bean Base (page 184), drained

large bunch of basil (about 30g/1oz), torn

small bunch of mint leaves (about 15g/½oz), roughly chopped

60g (2¼oz) rocket, or watercress and rocket salad mix

50g (1¾oz) vegetarian hard cheese or Parmesan, shaved

50g (1¾oz) toasted nuts of your choice (we love pine nuts, walnuts or hazelnuts)

sea salt

1 Trim the ends off the courgettes, then use a flat vegetable peeler to peel them lengthways into ribbons (a mandoline could also be used here, if you have one). Continue to peel until you reach the core of the courgettes. You may find this leaves a lot of courgette remaining, so see our Tip below for how to use this.

2 Place the courgette ribbons in a colander over a bowl. Season with salt and allow to stand for 2–3 minutes to draw out the excess water.

3 In a small mixing bowl, mix together the lemon juice, garlic, olive oil and vinegar. (Cut down on the balsamic if you don't like it too sharp, or add more lemon juice instead.)

4 Tip the courgette ribbons into a large serving bowl or platter and scatter over the lemon zest. Add the butter beans to the bowl, followed by the basil, mint and rocket and toss everything together.

5 Drizzle over the dressing and toss thoroughly to coat.

6 Finish by sprinkling over the cheese and toasted nuts, then serve.

Chop the courgette core left after making the ribbons and sauté over a medium heat in olive oil. Toss into the salad at the end for extra flavour.

This is speedy, crispy and crunchy: a great summer lunch when you're short of time but in need of something nourishing and delicious. It's a great way to use up any sad-looking courgettes in the fridge. We spotted this gem of a recipe on Beth Adamson's Instagram page. Also known as the Borough Chef, she's an incredible home cook, recipe developer and a true bean champ. If you enjoy this recipe, then check out page 142 for another of Beth's creations.

Feeds 2
Takes 10 minutes

FRIED BEANS + COURGETTES

3–4 tablespoons olive oil, plus extra to serve

700g (1lb 9oz) jar Queen Butter Beans, or 1 White Bean Base (page 184), drained

pinch of dried chilli flakes (optional)

2 large courgettes, sliced into rounds roughly 5mm (¼in) thick (try a mix of green and yellow courgettes, if you can get them)

3–4 thyme sprigs, leaves picked, or ½ teaspoon dried thyme

2 garlic cloves, thinly sliced

zest and juice of 1 large lemon

small bunch of parsley (about 15g/½oz), finely chopped

sea salt and freshly ground black pepper

1 Heat 2 tablespoons of the olive oil in a frying pan over a high heat. Add half the butter beans to the pan and cook, stirring occasionally, for about 4 minutes until golden and crispy. Transfer to a plate and repeat with the remaining butter beans; you may need to add another tablespoon of oil for the second batch if the pan gets dry. When all the beans are done, turn off the heat, then return the first batch to the pan. Sprinkle over the chilli flakes, if using, and set aside.

2 Meanwhile, heat 2 tablespoons olive oil in a frying pan over a low heat. Add the courgettes and sweat until starting to soften, then stir in the thyme and garlic and cook out for another 3–4 minutes.

3 Add the beans to the courgette pan, along with the lemon juice and parsley, and stir to combine. Season to taste and finish with lemon zest and an extra drizzle of olive oil to serve.

This recipe is such a great summery dish. It's perfect as a side to a barbecue, but tasty and hearty enough to hold its own as a lunch. The simplicity of the recipe allows the sumac-roasted chickpeas to shine through and take centre stage – we can almost guarantee there will be no leftovers. We first discovered this recipe through Tiggy Willett, one of Amelia's childhood friends, and knew a version of it had to be in the book. We've added petits pois to Tiggy's original recipe, which we love as it lightens it a little.

CHARRED COURGETTE + CHICKPEA SALAD WITH LEMONY YOGURT

Feeds 2–3
Takes 30–35 minutes

700g (1lb 9oz) jar chickpeas or 2 × 400g (14oz) cans chickpeas, drained

4 tablespoons olive oil

2 tablespoons sumac

3 courgettes, quartered lengthways then chopped into thirds

100g (3½oz) cooked petits pois (frozen are fine here)

2 Baby Gem lettuces

large bunch of mint (about 30g/1oz), leaves picked

1 teaspoon dried chilli flakes (optional)

sea salt and freshly ground black pepper

For the lemony yogurt dressing

juice of 1 lemon

3 tablespoons Greek, natural or plant-based yogurt

1 garlic clove, crushed

1 tablespoon olive oil

1   Preheat the oven to 200°C/180°C fan/400°F/gas mark 6.

2   Rinse the chickpeas, then tumble them into a roasting tray and pat dry with a paper towel. Drizzle with 2 tablespoons of the olive oil, then sprinkle over the sumac. Season with salt and pepper and toss well to coat. Roast for 25–30 minutes until golden and crisp.

3   Brush the courgettes with the remaining 2 tablespoons of olive oil and sprinkle over a good pinch of salt. Heat a griddle pan over a high heat and add the courgettes. Griddle for around 2 minutes on each side until nicely browned – you're looking for deep char marks here.

4   While the courgettes are cooking, make the dressing. Mix all the ingredients together in a small bowl and season to taste, adding more lemon if you like.

5   To assemble the salad, toss the charred courgettes, crispy chickpeas and lettuce leaves together in a large salad bowl, then drizzle over the yogurt dressing and sprinkle with fresh mint leaves. Add chilli flakes if desired for some heat and serve.

This speedy salad takes less than 10 minutes and still feels like a really indulgent feast. The white beans are smothered in a zesty dressing for a quick marinade, and then you just need to tear some mozzarella and mortadella, pop open a jar of artichokes, and you're basically there. You can omit the mortadella, and it will still be delicious. We like this acidic, to cut through the creamy cheese and salty mortadella, but taste as you go with the lemon if you feel this may not be to your liking, and adjust accordingly.

Feeds 2
Takes 10 minutes

MARVELLOUS MARINATED SALAD

700g (1lb 9oz) jar butter beans, or 1 Butter Bean Base (page 184), drained

1 garlic clove, crushed

zest and juice of 1½ lemons, or to taste

150g (5½oz) jarred artichokes in oil, drained, chopped into smaller pieces if they look too large

3 tablespoons extra virgin olive oil (see Tip below)

250g (9oz) mozzarella, torn into bite-sized pieces

4–5 slices of mortadella ham (about 80–90g/2¾–3¼oz), or any good-quality cold cut of ham, each slice torn into 4 pieces (optional)

large bunch of basil (about 30g/1oz), roughly chopped

50g (1¾oz) hazelnuts or pine nuts, lightly toasted, then chopped

2 butter lettuces, torn into bite-sized pieces (you want a lettuce that's soft but still able to hold its shape; if butter lettuce is hard to come by, go for a mix of Little Gem and rocket)

sea salt and freshly ground black pepper

1 Tip the beans into a large, shallow bowl. Add the garlic, lemon zest and juice, artichokes and olive oil. Give it a good stir, and season with plenty of black pepper.

2 Scatter the mozzarella on top and stir lightly again so that the cheese merges into the garlicky oil. Taste at this point and adjust the seasoning; it may need a pinch of flaky salt at this stage, or an extra squeeze of lemon.

3 Next, sprinkle over the mortadella, if using, along with the basil and toasted nuts. You can add the lettuce at this point, tossing the salad to combine, but if you're serving this at a dinner party, we suggest you plate up the lettuce first and spoon this heavenly mixture on top to keep things pretty.

If the olive oil from the jar of artichokes is high quality, then use this in place of the olive oil in the recipe to avoid waste.

BEAN FEASTS 6

Melissa Hemsley

The real win with this – and any – traybake is that you can bung it in the oven, whip it out after a while and serve directly in the tray, meaning minimal washing-up afterwards. To minimise your food waste, don't worry about peeling the sweet potatoes; just remove any real hefty knobbly parts.

SWEET POTATO, FETA + BLACK BEAN TRAYBAKE

Feeds 4
Takes 40 minutes

2 sweet potatoes, scrubbed and cut into wedges (or 1 small butternut squash)

4 tablespoons olive oil

1 tablespoon cumin seeds

6 spring onions, trimmed and cut into thirds (or 1 large red onion)

½ 700g (1lb 9oz) jar black beans, or 400g (14oz) can black beans, drained and rinsed

2 large handfuls of curly kale or cavolo nero (roughly 140g/5oz), torn into bite-sized pieces

200g (7oz) feta

sea salt and freshly ground black pepper

For the coriander-lime drizzle
large bunch of coriander (about 30g/1oz), finely chopped (save a few whole leaves for garnish)

1 jalapeño, deseeded if you prefer less heat, finely chopped (or 4–6 slices of pickled jalapeños)

zest of 1 lime and juice of 2

6 tablespoons extra virgin olive oil

To serve
your favourite tortillas, lime wedges

1   Preheat the oven to 220°C/200°C fan/425°F/gas mark 7.

2   In a large baking tray, toss the sweet potato wedges with 2 tablespoons of the olive oil. Scatter over the cumin seeds and season with sea salt and pepper, then spread out so that they're evenly spaced and not touching. This is important as you want them to roast rather than steam; use 2 trays if needed. Roast for 20 minutes.

3   After 20 minutes, turn the wedges, then add the spring onions and black beans to the tray. Drizzle with 1 tablespoon of the olive oil, and add another sprinkle of salt. Return the tray to the oven for 8–10 minutes until the spring onions have softened and caramelised.

4   Remove from the oven and add the kale to the tray. Drizzle with the remaining 1 tablespoon olive oil and roast for another 5 minutes until the kale is slightly crisp at the edges.

5   To make the drizzle, simply mix all the ingredients together in a bowl and season to taste.

6   When everything is ready, crumble the feta over the traybake and top with the reserved coriander leaves and about half of the drizzle. Serve with tortillas, lime wedges and the remaining drizzle for everyone to help themselves.

Feeds 4
Takes 1 hour 30 minutes

30g (1oz) butter, softened

3 fat garlic cloves, crushed

small bunch of thyme (about 15g/½oz)

1.5kg (3lb 5oz) whole free-range chicken

1 small lemon, halved

3 rosemary sprigs

1 fresh bay leaf

½ tablespoon flaky sea salt

1 tablespoon olive oil

For the beans

1 tablespoon olive oil

1 onion, finely chopped

20g (¾oz) butter

20g (¾oz) plain flour

300ml (10fl oz) hot chicken stock

700g (1lb 9oz) jar butter beans, with their bean stock, or 2 × 400g (14oz) cans butter beans, drained, with 200ml (7fl oz) chicken stock

30g Parmesan, finely grated

2 teaspoons white wine vinegar

1 teaspoon Dijon mustard

3 tablespoons double cream

1–2 tablespoons white truffle oil (depending on how much you love truffle!)

small bunch of tarragon (about 15g/½oz), finely chopped (optional)

sea salt and freshly ground black pepper

To serve

crusty bread and cooked green vegetables, such as hispi cabbage, cavolo nero or asparagus

Fat butter beans are a great vessel for soaking up flavours, and they turn this instantly into a complete meal. For extra-crispy skin, salt your chicken the night before. And for ultimate comfort, finish with the best truffle oil you can afford and a slick of cream. Grab a hunk of crusty bread for mopping.

CRISPY HERB-STUFFED CHICKEN WITH TRUFFLE BEANS

---

1   Preheat the oven to 240°C/220°C fan/475°F/gas mark 9.

2   In a small bowl, mash together the butter and garlic. Pick the leaves from half the thyme sprigs and mix those in too.

3   Set your chicken on a chopping board. Push your fingers between the skin and flesh of the chicken breasts, and push the butter and garlic mixture under the skin. Press the lemon, remaining thyme sprigs, rosemary sprigs and bay leaf into the cavity. Season the skin all over with the salt, and drizzle with the olive oil. Tie the legs together with string and transfer to a large roasting tray. Roast, uncovered, for 30 minutes.

4   To prepare the beans, heat the oil in a deep non-stick frying pan or saucepan over a low heat. Add the onion, along with a pinch of salt, and fry for 10–12 minutes, or until softened and translucent. Add the butter to the pan and, once melted, stir through the flour to make a roux. Cook for 2 minutes.

5   Add the chicken stock in several additions, stirring continuously until you have a thickened sauce. Add the beans and bean or chicken stock, and bring to a simmer, then stir through the Parmesan, white wine vinegar, mustard, cream and truffle oil. Season to taste.

6   One the chicken has had its 30 minutes, remove from the oven. Tip the beans into the roasting tray around the chicken. Reduce the oven temperature to 180°C/160°C fan/350°F/gas mark 4 and roast everything for a further 35 minutes, or until the juices run clear when you cut into one of the chicken legs. Leave to rest for 10 minutes.

7   Scatter the tarragon over the butter beans, then carve the chicken and serve with crusty bread and some green veg.

The easiest way to chop dried chillies is to snip them with kitchen scissors.

Smoky and rich molten black beans, loaded with cheese, served with a herby soured cream and quick pickled onions to cut through the richness. Ancho chillies are well worth seeking out; they are mild in heat but pack a punch when it comes to flavour. This dish is utterly satisfying as it is, but if you're feeling a wee bit greedier, serve with baked sweet potatoes.

Feeds 2–3
Takes 20 minutes

SMOKY BLACK BEAN BAKE

2 tablespoons extra virgin olive oil

5 garlic cloves, sliced

4 tablespoons tomato purée

1½ teaspoons smoked paprika

1 dried ancho or chipotle chilli, finely chopped (or ½ teaspoon dried chilli flakes or 1–2 teaspoons chipotle paste)

1 teaspoon ground cumin

700g (1lb 9oz) jar black beans with their bean stock, or 2 × 400g (14oz) cans black beans, drained, with 200ml (7fl oz) veg stock

180g (6¼oz) Cheddar, grated, or pre-grated mozzarella

sea salt and freshly ground black pepper

your favourite tortillas, to serve (optional)

For the quick pickled onion

1 red onion, halved and very finely sliced

zest and juice of 2 limes

squeeze of honey or agave

For the herby soured cream

4 tablespoons soured cream, crème fraîche or Greek yogurt

small bunch of coriander (about 15g/½oz), stalks and all

1   Preheat the oven to 220°C/200°C fan/425°F/gas mark 7.

2   To make the quick pickled onion, mix the onion slices with the lime juice and honey or agave in a small bowl. Season with a pinch of salt and set aside.

3   Heat the oil in an ovenproof saucepan over a medium–high heat. Add the garlic and fry for about 1 minute until lightly golden. Stir in the tomato purée, paprika, chilli and cumin (be careful of splattering), and fry for 30 seconds, reducing the heat as needed to prevent the garlic from burning.

4   Add the beans, along with their bean stock, and season with generous pinches of salt and pepper. You may need to add a splash of water here; you want it to have a molten, porridge-like consistency. Reduce the heat to low and simmer for 8–10 minutes until you achieve this.

5   If you're happy with the width of your pan, keep the mixture in there. If it's a little small, pour the mixture into a small, tall-sided baking tray, as you want enough surface area for the cheese to melt. Sprinkle the cheese evenly over the top, then bake for 5–10 minutes until the cheese has melted.

6   While the beans are cooking, put the soured cream and coriander into a food processor. Drain the lime juice from the pickled onions and pour that in too, then whizz until smooth. Season to taste.

7   When the beans are browned, leave to sit for a few minutes before serving in bowls or spooning on to soft tortillas. Dollop over the herby soured cream and pickled onions, and enjoy.

Joey O'Hare and Katy Taylor of Husk

Feeds 4
Takes 1 hour 15 minutes

For the rosemary roasted squash

4 rosemary sprigs, leaves finely chopped

1 small or medium-sized butternut squash or pumpkin (such as onion squash), skin on, chopped into 2cm (¾in) chunks

2 onions (red or white), sliced

2 tablespoons olive oil

sea salt and freshly ground black pepper

For the garlic cream cheese

1 garlic bulb

2 tablespoons olive oil

6 tablespoons full-fat cream cheese or plant-based alternative

juice of ¼ lemon

2 tablespoons double cream, yogurt or plant-based alternative

For the broth

2 tablespoons olive oil

1 onion (red or white), diced

2 celery stalks, sliced

2 carrots, chopped

1 leek, finely sliced

4 garlic cloves, sliced

2 anchovies (optional – if you don't use them, maybe bump up the salt)

200g (7oz) cavolo nero or kale, shredded

2 × 400g (14oz) cans chopped tomatoes

700g (1lb 9oz) jar butter beans with their bean stock, or 2 × 400g (14oz) cans butter beans with 200ml (7fl oz) extra veg stock

We have made countless versions of this bean stew, which is as versatile as can be. This version is an autumnal beauty that is both comforting and nourishing. We top it with a roasted garlic cream cheese, which adds huge depth of flavour, and a warm, punchy sage and walnut gremolata, which is both zingy thanks to a squeeze of lemon and deeply savoury from the toasted walnuts.

ROAST SQUASH RIBOLLITA

1 Preheat the oven to 190°C/170°C fan/375°F/gas mark 5. In a large roasting tray, toss the chopped rosemary with the squash, red onions and olive oil. Season with salt and pepper and spread out into an even layer.

2 Take the garlic bulb for the garlic cream cheese and rub away the external layer of skin. Carefully slice off the top of the bulb to expose the tip of each clove – this will make it easier to squish out the roasted garlic later on. Lightly rub with the olive oil, then wrap loosely in foil and pop on the roasting tray with the squash. Roast in the oven for 30 minutes.

3 Heat the oil for the broth in a large, heavy-based saucepan over a medium heat. Add the onion and sauté for 8 minutes until gently caramelised and soft. Add the celery, carrots, leek and garlic, with the anchovies, if using. Season with a pinch of salt. Continue cooking for a further 12 minutes, stirring often.

4 Add the cavolo nero, tomatoes and beans with their bean or veg stock. Season with salt and pepper, then cover with a lid. Reduce the heat to low and simmer for 20 minutes (you may need 10–15 minutes longer, and more salt, if using canned beans).

5 After 30 minutes of roasting, remove the squash and onions from the oven. Check the garlic; you want it to be soft, golden and oozing – if not, return to the oven for a further 15 minutes. Scatter the walnuts for the gremolata on to a separate baking tray and pop them in the oven for 4 minutes to toast.

6 Tip the roasted squash and onions into the broth. Continue to simmer very gently while you prepare the final bits.

7 Once the roasted garlic is ready, squeeze the cloves from their skins into

For the walnut + sage gremolata

40g (1½oz) walnuts, roughly chopped

4 tablespoons olive oil

16–20 sage leaves, finely sliced

1 small garlic clove

juice of ½ lemon

a bowl. Add the cream cheese, lemon juice and cream or yogurt, and a pinch of sea salt, then mash to combine.

8 To make the gremolata, heat the oil in your smallest frying pan over a low heat. Add the sage, garlic, walnuts and a pinch of salt, and sizzle very gently for 1 minute, just to take the raw edge off the garlic. Turn off the heat and squeeze in the lemon juice.

9 Serve in warmed bowls. topped with generous dollops of the zingy gremolata, and wonderfully enriching roasted garlic cream cheese.

Feeds 4
Takes 1 hour

500ml (17fl oz) whole milk

1 bay leaf (fresh or dried)

300g (10½oz) undyed smoked haddock fillet, skin removed

juice of ½ lemon

60g (2¼oz) butter

1 large leek, sliced

½ fennel bulb, finely chopped

50g (1¾oz) plain flour or gluten-free flour

50ml (2fl oz) white wine

¼ teaspoon grated or ground nutmeg

large pinch of cayenne pepper or hot chilli powder

large bunch of soft herbs (about 30g/1oz) – I like parsley, dill or tarragon, or a mix of all three, finely chopped

700g (1lb 9oz) jar Queen Butter Beans, or 1 White Bean Base (page 184), drained

180g (6¼oz) raw king prawns

2 tablespoons capers, drained

sea salt and freshly ground white pepper

For the crispy topping
100g (3½oz) breadcrumbs of your choice (fresh, gluten-free or panko)

40g (1½oz) Comté, finely grated (or Gruyère)

½ teaspoon smoked paprika

To serve (optional)
chopped chives, roe, such as trout or cod, cooked peas or greens

This warming, indulgent gratin screams comfort, while also being packed full of goodness, thanks to the butter beans. It's creamy, smoky and rich, with flaky white fish, smoked haddock, prawns and plump butter beans, and the Comté topping adds a nuttiness that really makes the dish feel luxurious. I love to serve it with buttered spinach and peas.

FISH PIE GRATIN

---

1   Preheat the oven to 200°C/180°C fan/400°F/ gas mark 6.

2   Pour the milk into a saucepan with the bay leaf and season with freshly ground pepper (I prefer white pepper with fish). Heat over a medium heat until steaming but not boiling, then add the smoked fish and poach for 3–5 minutes until just cooked. Remove with a slotted spoon to a plate and drizzle the lemon juice over the fish. Reserve the milky poaching liquor – you'll use this for your sauce.

3   Melt the butter in another large saucepan over a medium heat. Add the leek and fennel and season with salt and pepper. Fry for 6–8 minutes until softened and sweet but not colouring. Scatter over the flour, and stir to coat, creating a paste. Cook for a further minute, then slowly pour in the wine, stirring to form a thicker roux, followed by the poaching liquor. Whisk continuously with a balloon whisk to remove any lumps, until the sauce is smooth and thickened.

4   Reduce the heat slightly and cook, stirring gently, for about 3 minutes. Taste the sauce and season with nutmeg, cayenne and a little salt to taste. Add the fresh herbs and gently stir these through, followed by the beans, prawns and capers. Turn off the heat and allow to cool slightly, then flake the fish into the sauce, removing any bones, and stir to combine. Pour the mixture into an oven dish.

5   To make the topping, mix together the crumbs, cheese and paprika in a bowl, then scatter it evenly over the fish filling. Bake for 35 minutes, until the top is golden and the filling is bubbling. Allow to settle for 10 minutes, then scatter over the chopped chives, if using. Dish up, spooning over the roe (if using) to finish. Serve with wilted spinach or peas – chips wouldn't go amiss, either.

The oceanic salinity of sweet clams with the earthy funk of good jamón is a near-perfect marriage of flavours. Add a jar of creamy white beans, some finely chopped herbs and a good whack of lemon juice, and you'll have a table of very happy folks fighting over spent shells for the last mouthful.

CLAMS WITH JAMÓN, WHITE BEANS + SHERRY

Feeds 4
Takes 25 minutes

1kg (2lb 4oz) clams, or mussels to give this a moules marinière vibe (ditch the jamón in this case)

2 tablespoons olive oil

4 large shallots or 2 banana shallots, finely diced

2 fat garlic cloves, thinly sliced

180ml (6fl oz) Fino sherry

700g (1lb 9oz) jar white beans, or 1 White Bean Base (page 184), drained

120g (4¼oz) jamón ibérico, cut into slivers (or Parma ham or prosciutto)

100g (3½oz) butter

lemon juice, to taste

small bunch of chives (about 15g/½oz), chopped

small bunch of flat-leaf parsley (about 15g/½oz), chopped

sea salt and freshly ground black pepper

crusty bread or pan con tomate (toasted bread with grated tomato, olive oil and garlic), to serve

1 Rinse your clams in icy-cold fresh water to make sure they're sparkling clean. Drain and set aside.

2 Heat the olive oil in your biggest pot (make sure it's got a lid) over a low–medium heat. Chuck in the shallots, along with a tiny pinch of salt, and cook for 8–10 minutes until translucent.

3 Crank up the heat to medium-high and add your garlic. Cook for 1 minute more until fragrant, then chuck in the clams. Make sure your pan is hot, then add the sherry. Cover with the lid and give the whole lot a good shake.

4 As soon as your clams open up (this will take 3–4 minutes), remove them from the pan using a slotted spoon and pop them into a bowl, leaving the liquid in the pan. Ditch any clams that stay shut.

5 Chuck the white beans and jamón into the pan, then reduce the heat to low. Let the mixture bubble away for 5–10 minutes until the beans are hot.

6 Have a taste; the clams will have released a delicious liquor, and the beans will soak up all this flavour. If you need to add a splash of water to loosen things up, do so, then stir in the butter and season with lemon juice, salt and black pepper.

7 Return the clams to the pan and stir through the buttery sauce. Finish with the chopped herbs. Serve with crusty bread or pan con tomate, and a cold glass of cava. Get stuck in.

I'm all about comfort food, and there are few meals more comforting to me than a beany stew. This one is packed with soft leeks and juicy sausages, with a crispy sausage-fat pangrattato to finish. I add spinach for green-ness, but kale, chard or cavolo nero would also work. This is still a wonderful dinner with veggie alternatives, too.

Feeds 2–3
Takes 30 minutes

CREAMY SAUSAGE, LEEK + BEAN STEW

3 tablespoons olive oil

1 large leek, finely chopped

2 garlic cloves, crushed

4 thyme sprigs, leaves picked

150ml (5fl oz) white wine

150ml (5fl oz) chicken or veggie stock

700g (1lb 9oz) jar butter beans with their bean stock, or 2 × 400g (14oz) cans white beans with 200ml (7fl oz) chicken or veg stock

6 sausages of your choice (choose veggie sausages to make this veggie)

200g (7oz) spinach (or shredded kale or cavolo nero)

25g (1oz) breadcrumbs of choice (fresh, gluten-free or panko)

2 tablespoons crème fraîche (or soured cream or double cream with 1 teaspoon lemon juice)

20g (¾oz) Parmesan (or Pecorino, Grana Padano or veggie alternative, grated)

zest and juice of ½ lemon

steamed broccoli, to serve (optional)

sea salt and freshly ground black pepper

1 Heat 2 tablespoons of the olive oil in a large frying pan or casserole dish over a medium heat. Add the leek, along with a pinch of salt, and cook for 3–4 minutes until softened. Stir in the garlic and thyme leaves, then cook for a further 1–2 minutes.

2 Add the wine and stock, followed by the beans with their bean or veg or chicken stock. Stir to combine, then reduce the heat to low and cover with a lid. Simmer for 10–15 minutes if using jarred beans or 15–20 minutes if using canned beans, until the beans are turning soft.

3 Meanwhile, heat the remaining 1 tablespoon of oil in a frying pan over a medium heat. Add the sausages and cook for roughly 6–7 minutes until nicely charred on the outside.

4 Taste the bean mixture and season if necessary, then add the spinach and stir it through. Place the sausages on top of the mixture, then cover once more and cook for a further 6–7 minutes.

5 Meanwhile, chuck the breadcrumbs into the same frying pan the sausages were cooked in, and fry over a medium heat until lightly browned. The crumbs will soak up all of that good sausage flavour.

6 Remove the lid from the casserole dish and stir in the crème fraîche, Parmesan and lemon zest and juice, along with some cracked black pepper.

7 Spoon on to plates and sprinkle over the breadcrumbs to serve. This is great with steamed broccoli on the side.

This recipe isn't a quick fix, but like with any roast, cooking low and slow is seriously worth the melt-in-the-mouth outcome. It's rich, it's indulgent and it's a serious showstopper. The lamb is slowly braised in delicious Moroccan spices and citrus flavours, and the chickpeas add nuttiness and bite. Serve with a cooling mint yogurt to cut through the richness. Trust us, this will become your new Sunday roast tradition.

Feeds 6
Takes 4 hours–4 hours 30 minutes

MOROCCAN ROAST LAMB + CHICKPEAS

2kg (4lb 8oz) lamb shoulder, on the bone

1 tablespoon olive oil

100g (3½oz) runny honey (about 5 tablespoons)

5 fat garlic cloves, finely chopped

40g (1½oz) fresh ginger, grated

zest and juice of 2 lemons

zest and juice of 2 oranges

2 tablespoons ras el hanout (or a Lebanese or Moroccan spice mix)

500g (1lb 2oz) small onions or shallots, halved

150g (5½oz) raisins or sultanas

For the mint yogurt
4 tablespoons thick Greek yogurt, or dairy-free alternative

small handful of mint (about 15g/½oz), roughly chopped

For the saucy chickpeas
500ml (17fl oz) lamb or chicken stock

1½ tablespoons dark soy sauce or tamari

1 tablespoon tomato purée

2 × 700g (1lb 9oz) jars chickpeas or 2 × Chickpea Base (page 184), with their bean stock

1 Preheat the oven to 200°C/180°C fan/400°F/gas mark 6. Rub the lamb with salt and the oil, then roast, skin-side up, in a deep tin, for 35 minutes until golden brown. Remove from the oven and transfer to a plate or board. Reduce the heat to 160°C/140°C fan/325°F/gas mark 3.

2 Meanwhile, make the mint yogurt. Combine the yogurt and chopped mint in a small bowl and mix well, then set aside in the fridge.

3 In a separate small bowl, combine the honey, garlic, ginger, lemon and orange zest and juice, and the ras el hanout. Mix well.

4 Once the lamb is out of its initial cook and removed from the tray, scatter the halved onions and raisins into the roasting tin the lamb was cooked in. Pour the honey and citrus mixture over the top, toss everything to coat and place the lamb back in the centre of the tin. Cover tightly with foil, sealing carefully around the edges. Unless this is tight, the raisins may burn. Cook slowly for roughly 3½ hours.

5 When the lamb has 30 minutes left of cooking time, make your saucy chickpeas. Combine the stock, soy sauce and tomato purée in a saucepan over a medium heat. Bring to the boil and cook until the mixture has reduced by half, stirring occasionally. At this point, add the chickpeas with their bean stock. Simmer away for another 10 minutes, then keep warm.

6 After the meat has been roasting for 3½ hours, remove the foil – the lamb should fall apart effortlessly.

7 Increase the oven temperature to 200°C/180°C fan/400°F/gas mark 6. Baste the lamb with a little of its own cooking juices. If there aren't enough, add a few tablespoons of water and a couple of tablespoons of

To serve

70g (2½oz) flaked almonds, toasted

small bunch of coriander (about 15g/½oz), stalks and all, roughly chopped

green salad or steamed greens, such as broccoli (optional)

the juice from the saucy chickpeas. Return the lamb to the oven for 5–10 minutes until the top is nicely caramelised.

8 Remove the lamb from the oven and brush it with some of the juice from the saucy chickpeas to give it a glossy shine. Spread out the chickpeas on a wide serving platter, then lay the lamb on top. Scatter over the toasted almonds and chopped coriander. Serve with a dollop of the yogurt and aside of green leaves or steamed greens for freshness.

Alexandra Dudley

For a milder garlic flavour, roast the garlic first before blitzing it in the purée.

A dish that pops in both colour and flavour. The dip uses the best of the herb garden – parsley, mint and dill – and is fresh and zesty. I love this with acorn squash but onion squash and butternut work beautifully too. Do not skimp on the butter (if anything, make extra – you won't regret it!).

ROASTED SQUASH WITH CHILLI BUTTER + HERBY BEAN DIP

Feeds 3–4
Takes 45 minutes–1 hour

700g (1lb 9oz) jar white beans, or 1 White Bean Base (page 184), with their bean stock

1 garlic clove

small bunch of flat-leaf parsley (about 15g/½oz), chopped

30g (1oz) complementary soft herbs (I like dill and mint), chopped

juice of 2 lemons

4 tablespoons olive oil

2 small acorn squash (or 1 large butternut squash), deseeded and cut into wedges

sea salt and freshly ground black pepper

For the chilli butter

3 tablespoons olive oil

1 garlic clove, crushed

1 teaspoon dried chilli flakes, or to taste

40g (1½oz) butter or dairy-free alternative

50g (1¾oz) shelled pistachios, roughly chopped

1 tablespoon finely chopped mint leaves

1 Preheat the oven to 200°C/180°C fan/400°F/gas mark 6.

2 Add the beans and 4 tablespoons of their stock to a blender or food processor, along with the garlic, herbs, lemon juice and 3 tablespoons of the olive oil. Blend until smooth and check for seasoning, adding a splash of water to loosen if necessary.

3 Tumble the squash wedges onto a baking tray and drizzle with the remaining 2 tablespoons of olive oil. Season with salt and toss well to coat. Roast for 40 minutes until the squash is cooked through and slightly caramelised, turning halfway through to ensure each piece is evenly roasted.

4 To make the chilli butter topping, heat the olive oil in a small saucepan over a low–medium heat. Add the garlic and cook for 2–3 minutes until softened and fragrant, then stir in the chilli flakes. Add the butter and allow to melt, stirring gently. Once the butter has melted, add the chopped pistachios and continue to stir for another minute or so. Take the pan off the heat and stir through the chopped mint.

5 To serve, spoon the bean purée on to a large serving plate. Arrange the roasted squash on top and drizzle over the chilli, mint and pistachio butter. Enjoy.

If you don't have pumpernickel, use a rustic wholemeal loaf or rye bread. Drizzle with 1 teaspoon maple syrup to replicate the pumpernickel's natural sweetness.

Sweetness from the broccoli, creamy zing from the white beans and saltiness from the Pecorino cheese make this a real showstopper of a veg-centric dish, all topped off with an earthy pumpernickel crunch for added texture. It can be warm, it can be cold – it's up to you. If you're feeling like something warm, just ensure you add the lemon juice at the last minute to prevent the juices from turning bitter.

Feeds 2 as a main, 4 as a starter
Takes 25–30 minutes

ANCHOVY + BROCCOLI WHITE BEAN DIP

1 quantity of Lemony Bean Dip (base recipe, page 66), warm or cold

50g (1¾oz) vegetarian hard cheese or Pecorino, grated

sea salt and freshly ground black pepper

For the pumpernickel crunch

3–4 slices pumpernickel bread

25g (1oz) butter

1 teaspoon dried chilli flakes

For the broccoli

small head of broccoli, or 200g (7oz) long-stem broccoli, broken into bite-sized florets and stalk chunks

2 tablespoons olive oil

6 anchovies, roughly chopped

2 garlic cloves, minced

1 teaspoon dried chilli flakes

To serve

bread, such as extra pumpernickel or a rustic wholemeal loaf (optional), lemon wedges

1   Start by making the pumpernickel crunch. Whack the pumpernickel bread in the toaster for 4–5 minutes until toasted but not burned. Let it cool for a little, then blitz in a food processor until it forms chunky crumbs.

2   Melt the butter in a frying pan over a medium heat. Add the pumpernickel crumbs and chilli flakes, along with a pinch of salt. Cook for a few minutes until the crumbs are coated with butter and seasoning. Turn off the heat, but keep warm.

3   For the broccoli, put a large pot of salted water on to boil and get a bowl of ice-cold water ready. Blanch the broccoli in the boiling water for 3 minutes, then plunge into the icy water. Roughly chop into bite-sized chunks. Drain, then squeeze out any extra moisture.

4   Heat the olive oil in a frying pan over a medium heat. Add the anchovies, garlic and chilli flakes and fry for around 30 seconds until the anchovies have melted – make sure the garlic doesn't burn here. Add the broccoli to the pan, and stir to coat in the anchovy oil. Crank up the chilli flakes if you like it spicy.

5   Load this mixture on to the lemony bean dip, then sprinkle over the Pecorino cheese. Top with the pumpernickel crunch and give it a good grinding of black pepper. Serve with bread, if you like, and lemon wedges for the acid-lovers.

If using fresh basil, chop up the stalks and throw them into the pan with the garlic for extra flavour.

Rich, indulgent and oozing with cheese, this beanie bake has everything you love about a classic parmigiana – meltingly soft aubergine, gooey cheese – elevated with black beans, which add a rich texture and meatiness to the sauce. Pair with a fresh rocket salad to cut through the richness. The parmagiana can be prepared up to 3 days in advance and kept in the fridge until needed. If doing this, bake for an extra 15 minutes until piping hot and golden. This one freezes well, too.

Feeds 4
Takes 1 hour

BLACK BEAN PARMIGIANA

3 aubergines, sliced into 1cm (½in) rounds

4–5 tablespoons olive oil

2 garlic cloves, finely sliced

1 tablespoon tomato purée

¼ teaspoon ground cinnamon (optional)

2 × 400g (14oz) cans good-quality chopped tomatoes (or passata)

1 teaspoon white caster sugar

1 teaspoon dried chilli flakes (optional)

700g (1lb 9oz) jar black beans with their bean stock, or 2 × 400g (14oz) cans black beans, drained, with 200ml (7fl oz) veg stock

1 veggie stock cube (optional)

250g (9oz) mozzarella

100g (3½oz) vegetarian hard cheese or Parmesan

2–3 tablespoons shop-bought pesto (or be a whizz and whizz up your own), or a large bunch of basil (about 30g/1oz), optional (see Tip above)

sea salt and freshly ground black pepper

For the topping
100g (3½oz) breadcrumbs of your choice (fresh, gluten-free or panko)

1 Preheat the oven to 180°C/160°C fan/350°F/gas mark 4. Put the aubergine slices into a bowl, sprinkle generously with salt, toss to coat, then set aside for 10 minutes. (This reduces the bitterness, though many widely accessible newer varieties of aubergine don't have this bitterness, so you may not need to follow this step.)

2 Brush the aubergines with 2–3 tablespoons of the olive oil then arrange in a large roasting dish, covering the base. Roast for 20–30 minutes until are soft and golden (trust us, it's worth the wait). Remove from the oven.

3 Meanwhile, heat the remaining 2 tablespoons of olive oil in a saucepan over a medium heat. Add the garlic and fry for 1 minute, then add the tomato purée and cinnamon, if using, and cook for a further 2–3 minutes, stirring occasionally.

4 Pour the chopped tomatoes into the pan, along with the sugar (this cuts through the acidity of the tomatoes and allows a more balanced sauce). Add the chilli flakes, if using, and stir. Allow this to bubble for 4–5 minutes, then pour in the black beans, along with their bean or veg stock, crushing a few handfuls as you pour them in to thicken the sauce. Season to taste with salt and pepper. Simmer for about 10 minutes for jarred beans, and 12 minutes for canned, until it thickens into a rich sauce. Taste the sauce at this point; if you think it needs more depth and could do with some more salt, crumble the stock cube into the mix and let it dissolve.

5 To assemble, spread the sauce evenly over the aubergines, then tear the mozzarella over the top. Sprinkle over the hard cheese or Parmesan.

6 To make the topping, mix together the breadcrumbs and olive oil in a small bowl, along with the oregano, if using. Scatter this over the top and bake for 20–25 minutes until golden.

1 tablespoon olive oil

1 teaspoon dried oregano (optional)

For the rocket salad

juice of 1 lemon

2–3 tablespoons olive oil

60g (2¼oz) fresh rocket (or any salad leaves)

7 Meanwhile, make the salad. Combine the lemon juice, olive oil and a pinch of salt in a small mixing bowl. Stir to combine, then toss through the rocket. This dressing is sharp, which is how we like it, but feel free to add some sweetness if it's too much for you.

8 Once the bake is bubbling and oozing with cheese, remove from the oven. Allow to stand for a few minutes before tucking in. Dot with the pesto or tear over the basil leaves just before serving with the rocket salad on the side.

These literally go with anything and will work in any season. Roasting beans in oil means that they crack, they burst, they crisp up – in short, they taste absolutely incredible. With a similarly delicate flavour and soft centre to potatoes, these protein-filled bad boys are just as versatile, and far less faff, plus they will leave you feeling lighter.

Feeds 2–3 as a side
Takes 45 minutes

150ml (5fl oz) light oil, such as light olive, sunflower or rapeseed oil

700g (1lb 9oz) jar Queen Butter Beans or 1 White Bean Base (page 184), drained and rinsed

4 garlic cloves, bashed with the skins on (this will keep them from burning)

½ bunch of rosemary (10g/¼oz), leaves picked, or 2 teaspoons dried rosemary

CRISPY GARLIC ROASTED BUTTER BEANS

1 Preheat the oven to 200°C/180°C fan/400°F/gas mark 6.

2 Pour the oil into a roasting tray and place in the oven to heat for 5 minutes. This hot oil will help to create a beautiful crispy texture on your beans.

3 Meanwhile, pat the drained and rinsed butter beans dry using a piece of kitchen paper.

4 Take your hot oil out of the oven and carefully spoon the butter beans into the tray, being careful to avoid any spitting hot oil.

5 Add the garlic to the roasting tray, along with the rosemary, and roast for 30 minutes.

6 Remove from the oven and carefully turn the beans, then return to the oven and cook for a further 10 minutes, or until the beans are golden brown and crispy. Serve with the roasted garlic in their skins, making it optional to squidge out the caramelised centres.

• Serve with a whole roasted chicken.

• Enjoy with tzatziki and grilled meat.

• Use as a crispy topper for the Pea, Mint and Feta Smash on page 40.

Mash, the only reasonable accompaniment to a sausage. Remix as you please; make it garlicky, or cheesy. We've got our fave version here, which is flavoured with mild French mustard. Without any need for boiling, this can be ready faster than your bangers.

Feeds 2–3 as a side
Takes 10 minutes

CREAMY WHITE BEAN MASH

50g (1¾oz) butter or plant-based alternative

700g (1lb 9oz) jar white beans, or 1 White Bean Base (page 184), drained

1–2 tablespoons whole milk or plant-based alternative (optional)

1 tablespoon Dijon mustard

sea salt and freshly ground black pepper

1 Melt the butter in a saucepan over a medium heat. Add the beans, along with half of their stock. Cover with a lid and simmer for 5 minutes.

2 Remove from the heat and mash with a potato masher or blitz with a handheld blender to your desired consistency. Check the consistency of the mixture. If it's looking a bit thick, loosen with the optional milk and simmer for 1 minute more, then remove from the heat and add the Dijon. Taste and add salt and pepper, if necessary. Serve.

- Pair with bangers and red wine gravy.
- Serve topped with mushrooms in a creamy marsala sauce.

BIG BEANS BEST

Although this may turn out a little more like a gratin, due to the difficulty of layering butter beans, we needed to convey just how classy this gal can be. Paired with a slow-cooked hunk of meat or garlic mushrooms, we love to share this with friends and family on a cold winter's day.

Feeds 8–10 as a side
Takes 45 minutes

BUTTER BEAN DAUPHINOISE

250ml (12fl oz) whole milk

250ml (8fl oz) double cream

3 garlic cloves, peeled and left whole

½ bunch of thyme (about 10g/¼oz)

3 × 700g (1lb 9oz) jars Queen Butter Beans or 3 × Butter Bean Bases (page 184), drained

150g (5½oz) Gruyère or Comté, grated

sea salt and freshly ground black pepper

1 Preheat the oven to 200°C/180°C fan/400°F/gas mark 6.

2 Combine the milk, cream, garlic cloves and thyme in a large saucepan over a medium heat. Bring to a simmer. After 10 minutes of simmering, scoop out and discard the thyme and garlic. Season the sauce well with salt and cracked black pepper. Take a couple of handfuls of your beans and break them up using your hands (or mash with a fork), then add them to the sauce along with half of the grated cheese to thicken it slightly.

3 In a large baking dish, begin layering the drained beans. The aim is to create about 4 layers of butter beans here, so selecting a dish with good depth is key.

4 Once you have arranged your first layer of butter beans, pour over just enough garlic-infused cream to cover, but not so much that they are soaked. Keep layering beans and cream in this manner until you have filled the baking dish. After the final layer, top with the cheese.

5 Bake for 25–30 minutes until the cheese is golden and bubbling, then serve.

- Serve as a side to your favourite roast.
- Pair with salmon, mushroom or beef Wellington.

BIG BEANS BEST

Potato salad, the 70s classic: it may conjure up memories of terrible barbecues and canteen salads, or it may just be your fave accompaniment to charred sausages and park picnics. Whatever your previous perception, using beans to replace the potatoes in this dish is a winner; it's lighter, brighter and, well, better. Add lardons, charred asparagus or whatever you fancy. We love adding radishes to make the dish pop and add that essential crunchy freshness.

Feeds 3–4
Takes 20 minutes

WHITE BEAN 'POTATO' SALAD

2 teaspoons wholegrain mustard

1 tablespoons white wine vinegar

700g (1lb 9oz) jar Queen Butter Beans or 1 Butter Bean Base (page 184), drained

2–3 tablespoons good-quality mayonnaise

2 tablespoons crème fraîche or full-fat Greek yogurt

3 spring onions, thinly sliced

2 tablespoons capers and/or gherkins, chopped

about 40g (1½oz) fresh herbs – we suggest a mixture of chives, parsley, mint and chervil – finely chopped

100g (3½oz) radishes, sliced

sea salt

1 In a large bowl, whisk together the mustard and vinegar with a pinch of salt. Add the butter beans and give them a stir so that they begin to marinate.

2 Tip the mayonnaise into a separate mixing bowl and stir in the crème fraîche, spring onions, capers and three-quarters of the chopped herbs. Drain off any remaining vinaigrette from the butter beans and toss them into this mayonnaise mixture. Stir to combine.

3 Garnish with the remaining herbs and the radishes, and serve.

• Makes a great barbecue side dish.

• Serve alongside a whole roasted fish.

• Perfect for picnics.

All About the Base

One of the beautiful things about beans is that there are so many different kinds. The diversity of the legume family make them crucial to our future food system, as they offer food security (see page 6), but this also means that understanding how to use each variety can be something of a minefield. For most of the recipes in this cookbook, substituting one bean for another will work perfectly well – they all typically have a gentle flavour and soft texture – but if you're feeling a bit lost by that endless scope for exchange, we've given some recommendations here that will give you a closer fit. If the bean you have isn't on this list, look into what family the bean comes from. The coco de paimpol bean, for example, is part of the haricot family, and it can be used in any recipe calling for white beans.

BIG BEANS BEST. Sometimes we may mark a recipe with 'BIG BEANS BEST'; this is where the recipe needs the texture and weight of a larger variety of bean. Often, the size and texture is more important than their subtle flavours, so if we ask for big butter beans, then giant, kabuli-style chickpeas will still do.

 ## ADZUKI

Big in Japan and China, these small red beans have a slightly sweeter taste than your standard kindey beans. They even get used in desserts!

Use these in any recipe calling for red or black beans like Melissa's Black Bean Traybake on page 154.

 ## BLACK BEANS BLACK TURTLE BEANS

Similar to a red bean, these beans have a dark earthiness that often needs lifting with a zippy yogurt or some acidity from citrus (try them in our Furious Fennel + Black Bean Salad on page 134). They are mostly associated with Mexican cuisine and offer a great balance to fresh, crunchy ingredients like lettuce and sweetcorn.

We call directly for black beans in this book, but you can also use them in red bean recipes, as they can match the meatiness and can take on a similar level of spice.

BLACK-EYED BEANS COWPEAS, BLACK-EYED PEAS

While most 'beans' we think of hail from the Americas, this 'cowpea' comes from Africa. This almost-minerally tasting bean has a nice bite to it alongside its mild flavour.

You could use these in any of the white bean recipes, but they'll work better in dishes where the beans are left whole. This not only makes the most of the texture of the bean, but also means you can see the pretty black dots that give this bean its name.

BORLOTTI CRANBERRY

This is the pinto's more elegant, refined cousin: the fashionable borlotti. It is similarly chalky in texture yet mild in flavour, with a sweet and nutty undertone. If you can get them fresh, do it, and enjoy them simply cooked with some bay, garlic and herbs.

Avoid using them as chickpea replacements but go wild with subsituting the Borlotti's in any of our white bean recipes as they''ll be fully appreciated when used in less rich flavour combinations. They're a fan favourite used whole in recipes like our Marvellous Marinated Salad on page 151 or the Pasta e Fagioli on page 118.

BUTTER BEANS LIMA

While these aren't in the white haricot family, their flavour is very similar. You only need to look at their name to find the real difference: butter. These beans are richer and creamier, and with their bigger, flatter form, they have the ability to dominate a dish.

A dependable bean, these can be used in any white bean recipe in the book as they have the ability to both hold shape and give that neutral, creamy texture that's so delicious when blended. We also have recipes dedicated to them where their big size really shines (see the Crispy Garlic Roasted Butter Beans on page 176).

CANNELLINI

These have a nutty flavour and tender flesh, and are often used in Italian dishes like minestrone. The big sister of the white haricot family, these are one of the longest varieties and they hold their shape super well. This makes them great for dishes where the texture of the bean is more of a feature, such as salads.

You can use these in any white bean recipe in the book, but also venture into recipes where we call for Queen Butter Beans. While the size of the bean won't be as generous, they're one of the best subs for butter beans due to their larger size and similar flavour profile compared to others in the haricot family. Try them in the Ricotta + Pesto Butter Beans on page 77.

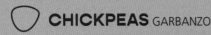

CHICKPEAS GARBANZO

There are many chickpea varieties – small ones, big ones, black ones – but they all give that nutty taste unmatchable with other beans – and God, we love them. A key ingredient in Mediterranean, Middle Eastern and Indian cuisines, you'll see chickpeas in traditional dishes across the world. Their strong flavours make them great to use in salads as they need little adding to them – THEY do the talking. And, of course, we don't need to tell you: hummus.

Their nutty, distinct taste make them tricky to interchange; we recommend sticking to recipes solely calling for a chickpea unless they're showing up in a dish where the sauce dominates the flavour (such as the Turkish-Style Eggs + Harissa Beans on page 18).

FAVA BEANS BROAD BEANS

We're big fans of this bean – it's meaty, with a thick skin, but brings a nuttiness that is oh-so-subtle. It's also a bean that can grow on British soil, which makes us love it even more.

You can find them split upon purchase due to how they are processed after harvest. In this format, they quite quickly break down, so it's important to use them in soups or dips where the bean is blended (try them in the Black Garlic Dip with Feta + Herb Yogurt on page 72). Or, if you've got hold of some whole dried favas, they can work well in place of red and black beans in dishes such as the Crispy Beans with Creamed Corn + Jalapeño Salsa on page 108.

FLAGEOLET

These are mild green beans that are actually young haricot beans picked before they're fully ripened and dried in the shade to retain their beautiful pale green colour. They're creamy like their mature sister bean, but unlike the haricot, they have an ability to retain their shape very well. This means they THRIVE in a slow cook where you want the bean kept whole for a bit of bite.

Use in any recipe calling for white beans, but save them for dishes where they're left whole, such as Ali's French Onion White Bean Bake on page 112.

HARICOT NAVY, ALUBIA BLANCA

We'll call this the OG white bean. Cannellini, alubia blanca, navy – they all stem from the mother of all: haricot beans. Creamy and starchy with a mild taste, these beans are great at absorbing the flavours of a dish and really shine when it comes to dips, mashes and stews as they break down easily, allowing them to thicken watery broths into creamy sensations.

Use these in any recipe that calls for white beans, but they perform best when allowed to mash or melt into the dish, such as our Lemony Bean Dip – 3 Ways on page 66.

PINTO PAPALOQUELITE, PERUANO

One of the most popular beans in Northern Mexico and the Southwestern United States, pinto beans are most often eaten whole, or mashed and then refried. This bean is arguably one of the most versatile. We see it sitting in the middle of the white, black and red bean families, as it's still mild in flavour, but it has an earthiness that can take on spices and richer stews.

You could probably use this bean in any recipe other than those asking for chickpeas, but they're likely to perform best when replacing black beans, so try them in the Smoky Black Bean Bake on page 159.

 QUEEN BUTTER BEANS JUDIONES, GIGANTES, ROYAL CORONAS, PIEKNY JAS, SCARLET RUNNER BEANS

When you try one of these we dare you not to say "that's the best butter bean I've ever tasted" (that's why this bean is our bestseller!), however, reading the small print you'll be suprised to hear they aren't techinically butter beans. They have a different Latin name entirely, along with thinner skins, creamier centres and a more time-consuming harvest.

Use them in any white bean or butter bean recipe and it will simply take the dish up a notch. The butter beans we sell at Bold Bean Co are of this kind – once you go big, there's no going back.

 **RED BEANS** RED KIDNEY BEANS, RED HARICOT BEANS, CHILLI BEANS

These are most commonly used in chilli con carne and in Indian dishes (where they're known as rajma). Their deep, earthy flavour and dark colour give a super-meaty vibe (try them in the Red Bean Ragu with Ricotta + Parmesan on page 174). They have a slightly thicker skin, which means they work well in slow-cooked stews where you want the beans to hold their shape.

We refer directly to these bright beauties in this book, but use them as a substitute for black beans such as Darina's Oaxacan-Style Salad on page 132.

Bold Bean Co beans taste a million miles better than what people have experienced before. We do this by choosing heirloom varieties and selecting the best grade of beans from each harvest. But how do we show that to the non-bean-believers? Rather than trying to communicate all of that on our labels, we decided to use 'Queen' as a stamp of our sourcing standards; we won't launch a new bean, unless it's a QUEEN!

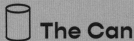

The Jar

We sell our beans in glass jars because the process of canning in glass cooks the beans at a lower temperature, better preserving the flavour and texture. While you can't guarantee that all jarred bean brands are going to source the same quality raw ingredients as us, buying beans in a jar will certainly beat a can in most cases.

Our jars are filled with the beautiful bean stock created in the cooking process, an ingredient we use in many of the recipes in this cookbook. Depending on the starch levels of a bean, some stocks can be thicker than others

– either way, treasure this stuff, its delicious. We also season our beans with the perfect level of salt during the cooking process, bringing out their natural flavour. While most other jarred bean brands include salt too, the levels will vary, so adjust to your preference and season your dishes to taste.

Some things to watch out for when buying jars: check for additives, as well as e-numbers and sulphites; these will all impact the bean stock. Try and find brands who are committed to quality in their sourcing.

The Can

Pulses have been commodified over the years and the most common format sold, cans, have seen the result of that, so can let the bean team down when it comes to flavour and texture. However, cans are sometimes all you have access to, so we've got a nifty hack you can use when cooking them: what we call a 'bean base' which is a way to get your cans as close to our jars as possible.

There are recipes where we don't call for a bean base, and instead you can use canned beans as they are. With

an extra 20 minutes spent bubbling in flavourful broths (such as the Cacio e Pepe Beans on page 111), canned beans will become more tender and closer in texture to jarred beans. In other recipes where beans are roasted (such as the Caramelised Cauliflower Chickpeas on page 142), the softer, bigger varieties in jars will have a more layered texture (crunchy on the outside, soft on the inside), but where the beans are providing crunch, this feature isn't fundamental.

BEAN BASE FOR CANNED BEANS

Makes 1 bean base

2 × 400g (14oz) cans beans (choose the variety based on the type of jarred bean suggested)

1 teaspoon bicarbonate of soda (baking soda)

1 teaspoon salt (if needed)

If the recipe requires bean stock

¼ stock cube, crumbled

150ml (5fl oz) boiling water

1 Pour the beans, along with their water, into a large saucepan. Add the bicarb. Then, check the labels on the tins; does the ingredients list include salt? If not, add the salt to the pan too.

2 Place over a medium-high heat and bring to the boil, then reduce the heat to low and simmer for 15 minutes until the beans have softened. Drain the beans and rinse.

3 Check the recipe you intend to use; does it require bean stock? If so, in a bowl, mush up ½ tablespoon of the beans with the stock cube. Pour the boiling water into the bowl and mix well so that the stock dissolves. Your recipe may tell you to add the beans and the stock together; in this case, you can simply add the drained beans to the bowl of stock until needed. Otherwise, store them separately and use as per the recipe's instructions. Your bean base is ready!

Dried Beans

Cooking beans from scratch is almost like a meditation; we encourage all of you to try it. With the ability to season throughout the cooking process, you can flavour the stock in subtle ways, adding depth and aromatics and taking it to the next level. However, while you should check out some of the recipes for brothy beans out there, we're here to make your life easier when cooking from this book, so we're giving you a simple recipe to elevate your dried beans to the same level as those in our beautiful jars – what we call a bean base.

Every batch of beans you buy will cook differently, as will every variety. Black beans and chickpeas tend to need a longer cooking time than white beans. Newly harvested beans require less cooking time and are often tastier. Older beans cook less evenly and are more likely to turn into mush.

Try and find a large, wide casserole pan with a heavy bottom – a shallow layer of beans means that the bottom layer doesn't get crushed, you want the beans whole.

BEAN BASE FOR DRIED BEANS

Makes 1 bean base

200g (7oz) dried beans (choose the variety based on the type of jarred bean suggested)

2 teaspoons fine sea salt

Soak:

Soak the beans overnight in 2 litres (3½ pints) of water. If left any longer, they'll begin to sprout. The next morning, drain and wash the beans to remove the antinutrients (which will also help reduce gas!). Fill a pot with 1.5 litres (2¾ pints) cold water and add the beans (unless they are chickpeas*). The water should be a couple of centimetres (an inch) above the beans.

Cook:

Place the pot over a medium-high heat and bring to the boil. Remove the initial scum as it could contain impurities. After that, any foam is natural and is simply the starches dancing in the water released from the beans. Try not to move the beans around too much, as this can break them down. Always keep at least 1–2cm (½–¾in) of water above the beans in the pan, otherwise the beans will become crowded, so top up with cold water as needed. When the beans are beginning to soften, add the salt. Salting them at this stage prevents the skins from hardening and coming off the beans.

As a starting point, cook the beans for at least 1½ hours. Some will require up to 2 hours. Keep checking towards the end; you want the beans to be tender but still firm.

Chickpeas are more delicate than other beans, so bring the water to the boil and add the chickpeas once boiling. This helps them stay tender, without breaking apart.

To create a bean base, add all of the cooked dried beans, along with 150ml (5fl oz) of their bean stock to a bowl or a container, or add directly to your chosen recipe. In some recipes, you won't need the stock, but don't discard it, or any leftover bean stock you have created, as you can use it as veg stock in any other dish! If you make multiple batches, these will freeze well in bags or airtight containers.

CONTRIBUTORS

THE BEAN CHAMPS

These incredible contributing chefs have supported our mission from day one and taken part by consistently inspiring us with bean recipes. They are at the forefront of our food culture, and we hope that, with them included, you'll see that it's not just a mad bunch of bean fanatics behind this book, but great foodies with great taste.

BETH ADAMSON
We have seen Beth (known as the Borough Chef) sky-rocket to fame in the last few years with her simple home cooking that celebrates great seasonal veg in an accessible way. She's been a big Bold Bean believer, and we love her for that. When our beans show up in her recipes, we know we're in for a treat. (Recipe on p. 142.)

DARINA ALLEN
Darina Allen started the world-famous Ballymaloe cookery school in Ireland, whose alumni have become renowned across the globe for their produce-led approach to cooking. (Recipe on p.132.)

ROSIE BIRKETT
Rosie is a food writer and columnist living in Kent. She celebrates seasonal British foods and is often drawn to seafood dishes inspired by her coastal surroundings. Whenever she features a bean in her dishes, we get very excited and quickly get to the kitchen. (Recipe on p.162.)

FLORENCE BLAIR
Florence and I connected very early on in the Bold Bean Co journey. We met up in a café in north London and struggled to stop talking. Without many people realising, she's behind the scenes in the work of many famous chefs, writing recipes and supporting cookbook shoots as a food and prop stylist. We were even lucky enough to bag her as a prop stylist for this book's shoot. (Recipe on p.90.)

OLIVIA CAVALLI
Olivia is a chef and food writer from London. She learnt to cook from her Italian nonna and her Italian heritage runs through all of her seasonal recipes. (Recipe on p.130.)

ESTHER CLARK
Esther has used our beans in dishes that make us drool, and we've been obsessed with the way she writes and styles her recipes for years. When asked who may be able to style this book, we immediately thought of Esther, but convinced ourselves she'd probably be booked up already. Somehow, she was free and willing (she does love beans, to be fair), so all of the beautiful dishes you see on these pages have her magic touch. She's a very special part of this book, so her very special recipe is fitting. (Recipe on p.156.)

HENRY DIMBLEBY AND JANE BAXTER
Henry Dimbleby is a huge mover and shaker in food sustainability in the UK. As the founder of healthy fast-food chain Leon, he's proved how good-quality, nutritious food can be made accessible. He sits on the board for the UK's Department for Environment, Food + Rural Affairs (Defra) and co-founded Chefs in Schools, a programme aimed at getting school children to eat more healthily and sustainably. I've admired his work for years, so when I saw his name come through as a subscriber to our monthly bean boxes, I yelped in excitement. It felt like a missed opportunity not to ask him to contribute a recipe to the book. He created the one in this book with his long-time collaborator Jane Baxter. (Recipe on p.64.)

ALEXANDRA DUDLEY
Alexandra is an amazing food writer and podcaster who has a real passion for hosting, food and sustainable living. She often uses our beans in her recipes, managing to make simple dishes feel like wondrous things you just want to share with people. (Recipe on p.171.)

HUGH FEARNLEY-WHITTINGSTALL
I met Hugh through a fellow foodie-founder friend called Tom, whose company 9 Meals from Anarchy makes the most beautiful organic stock pastes (I call them Nature's MSG; go find them if you're based in the UK). Speaking to Hugh, who has shaped so much of the food culture in the UK, was incredible, but what excited me even more was his enthusiasm around what we were doing. (Recipe on p.29.)

XANTHE GLADSTONE
Xanthe is a grower, food writer and food-sustainability advocate who lives in North Wales. She was one of the first people I told about my decision to begin Bold Bean Co, and as a big lover of beans herself, she couldn't have been more supportive. Xanthe uses seasonality to drive her recipes, so it seemed very apt to have a summer broth. (Recipe on p.98.)

SOPHIE GODWIN
Soph is the genius behind many incredible cookbooks – and, we're proud to say, even this one. As soon as we heard we were going to have this opportunity, she was our first port of call. She understands recipe-writing like no one else, and we knew that having her in our midst would make these recipes bullet-proof. She made us feel calm in times of panic, guided us through the process and, to top it off, is a huge inspiration in the kitchen. (Recipe on p.101.)

MELISSA HEMSLEY
If you follow Melissa, you'll know it's impossible not to be cheered up by her enthusiasm for beautiful food. Every now and then, you'll see a photo of her wide smile, offering you a bowl groaning with deliciousness, texture and colour – in almost all cases, they feature beans. (Recipe on p.154.)

COLU HENRY
Colu is a serious bean-lover and incredible chef from New York. We've watched her from across the pond for years, and this year we were put in touch by a mutual friend (thank you, Georgie!) to discuss all things beans – she's a true bean champ. We're thrilled to have her recipe in the cookbook. (Recipe on p.52.)

TOM HUNT
Tom Hunt is also known as the 'Eco Chef', and I've not met another food writer who could better deserve this name. Sustainability feeds into absolutely everything he does, and his recipes educate, excite and make you hungry for a new world. Tom is a big player in the Chefs' Manifesto, a community of chefs supported by the UN who are pushing the 'Beans is How' campaign (see

page 6). He champions beans not just for their flavour, but also because of the crucial role they play in a sustainable food system. (Recipe on p.19.)

BECK JOHNSON
Beck is based in Manchester, where she whips up seductive dishes that make you immediately hungry. She's been supporting us on our journey of making the world love beans from day one, and we are so excited to have her banger of a recipe in the mix for you. (Recipe on p.141.)

ANNA JONES
Anna has played a huge role in reducing my meat consumption. My house of girlfriends at university would all cook together, and time after time, we'd come back to Anna's books. She has brought a vibrancy and satisfaction to vegetarian cooking that has undoubtedly influenced our cooking style. Before we even launched Bold Bean Co, Anna shared what we were doing in her newsletter. She's been a huge support and we're thrilled that she could contribute a recipe to this book. (Recipe on p.84.)

GEORGIA LEVY
Georgia is a food writer based in London. She is a wonder in the kitchen, and her food so often celebrates veg in a generous but elegant way. Her recipe in this book demonstrates her approach perfectly. (Recipe on p.78.)

BEN LIPPETT
Ben is a chef who has worked in top London restaurants and written for MOB Kitchen, while also running a hot honey company (Dr Stings – try it on pizza and you'll never look back). His dishes have a real sophisticated edge, and his recipe in this book is

no exception. It will impress absolutely everyone – it's outrageously good. (Recipe on p.164.)

GILL MELLER
I first spoke to Gill Meller when working with suppliers of restaurants in my old job. An ex-River Cottage chef, he's produce-led, with a real passion for sustainability – so, naturally, he too has a bean obsession. He actually makes his dish outside in nature, over a hot fire in a cast-iron pan. Warm bowls of his beany broth would even make a cold, rainy day charming. (Recipe on p.92.)

THOMASINA MIERS
The incredible Thomasina Miers, chef, writer, and founder of Mexican restaurant, Wahaca, champions the bean in so many of her recipes, and she has kindly shared a hearty number that celebrates all things sweet, spicy and beany. (Recipe on p.88.)

Mob
The Mob team loves the bean. They have many bean recipes on their website (try the black bean and chorizo toastie for a real win), but the one here, by their bean queen, Sophie Wyburd, is our favourite, and they kindly let us include it in this cookbook. (Recipe on p.68.)

JOEY O'HARE AND KATY TAYLOR OF HUSK
Joey and Katy live on the Suffolk coastline, feeding people with their veg-centric dishes and teaching them how to cook in a mindful but majorly flavourful way. (Recipe on p.160.)

NISHA PARMAR
HANNAH: Nisha and I met through our love for food. I was inspired by her talents and love for Indian-style cooking, and I knew she would be the star

choice to whip up a fab bean dish celebrating this cuisine. Following her MasterChef success, Nisha has launched her own London café and become one of the most popular names in celebrity private dining, but nothing makes her happier than creating and enjoying delicious meals with her family. (Recipe on p.120.)

GRACE REGAN
Grace has used our beans everywhere from festivals in Wales to her much-loved Spice Box restaurant in Walthamstow. She's written cookbooks and has recently started selling delicious dahls in grocery stores. We're both pulse-mad foodies, and her incredible use of spice meant we had to have her contribute to this book. (Recipe on p.70.)

KLARA RISBERG
Klara may be the food world's best-kept secret. She is Swedish born, and her food has a real comfort to it. Her recipe in this book, which she allowed us to share on our website from our early days, is still one of the most loved in our community. (Recipe on p.111.)

ELENA SILCOCK
Elena is a food stylist and writer from London who has written for the likes of BBC Good Food and MOB Kitchen. Her newsletter, 'You Bring the Wine', centres around cooking for friends and has featured the bean far too many times for us not to fall in love with her. She celebrates beans in a simple but elegant way, as her dish in this book shows. (Recipe on p.99.)

ALI SLAGLE
Ali Slagle is a food writer from Brooklyn who writes frequently for the New York Times. If you don't already know how much of a bean-lover she is, just take

a look at her last book, *I Dream of Dinner*; it contains so many enticing recipes that it was very hard to choose our favourite. (Recipe on p.112.)

CLAIRE THOMSON
Claire, creator of the 5 O'clock Apron, is the tomato queen. She brings the love to the tomato, like we do to the bean, so this combination seemed like a very fitting recipe for her contribution to the cookbook. Claire's recipes are built around real life – like cooking for three hungry kids – making her food fuss-free, but with zero compromise on deliciousness. (Recipe on p.33.)

JOE WOODHOUSE
Joe is a food photographer and writer who is transforming perceptions around vegetarian cooking with his inventive, celebratory approach. It's actually thanks to him that we are even doing this book, as he introduced us to our now-agent – the fab Emily – who believed in the potential of this project. We are obsessed with Joe and can't quite believe we were lucky enough to have him shoot this book. His understanding of flavour and texture seeps through into the way he captures food. By flicking through this cookbook, you'll be able to appreciate how he brings the dishes alive. (Recipe on p.30.)

SOPHIE WYBURD
Soph continuously waxes lyrical about beans, and has already done so much for changing perceptions. We are endlessly grateful to her, and obsessed with her recipes. Her dish is a case in point – and make sure you also try her carrot, feta and chickpea number on page 68. (Recipe on p.167.)

THE BOLD BEAN TEAM

THE BEAN TEAM

Although I started this journey alone, our team has grown significantly. This book wouldn't be possible without the effort from the Bold Bean team, working tirelessly to make you obsessed with beans by giving you the best of beans. We now have my co-founder Ed (who makes everything run smoothly), Rosa (who perfects our products), Lucy and, most importantly for this cookbook, Hannah. Hannah can be found at @hans.hungry, the Instagram account where she excites and inspires followers with her fresh and filling recipes centred around taste. It was her extreme love of flavour and food – and, of course, her love of the bean – that meant we had to have her in the Bold Bean Team. This book has come together through endless brainstorming sessions, kitchen experiments and discussions around how we love lemon and cheese too much. While Hannah and I have been at the helm, it took a whole crew of bean champs to get us here.

Florence Haddock

Jo Parsons

Josephine King

Carl and Stephen Blades

Stephen Christie-Miller

Hester Rowell

Dean Phillips

Laura Verrecchia

Alex Hughes

Lizzie Christie-Miller

Sarah Whitehead

Deborah Tayler

From left to right
Hannah, Lucy, Amelia, Rosa + Ed.

Esther Clark + Caitlin Macdonald

Thank you to Soph
Godwin and Georgina
Cranston for their
editing, the wonderful
team that helped to
shoot and design the
book (Joe Woodhouse,
Juliette Norsworthy,
Emma Hanson, Esther
Clark, Caitlin Macdonald,
Florence Blair), Emily
Sweet and Judith Hannam
for believing in us to even
create this book and on a
personal level, I want to thank
my partner Fred for his patience
and support, and continuous
consumption of beans.

THE BEAN BUDS

Every week, we would send out our new recipe creations to a group of volunteers, our bean buds, who would test, perfect and critique the dishes. We really couldn't have done it without them. They have offered us a refreshing side salad where things got too rich, and became crucial to our recipe-writing process. They are the authors of this book just as much as we are.

Alex Hughes
Alex Whelpton
Alexia Auersperg-Breunner
Anne-Marie Egan
Andrew Hindley
Anna Harris-Noble
Annabelle Davis
Arabella Kennard
Belinda Barrow
Belle Seery
Brian Cross
Carl Blades
Carol Street
Carol White
Caroline Parkinson
Carolyn Arber
Charlie Whelpton
Charlotte Humphery
Clare Hughes
Clare Leeming
Clare Ronay
Daisy Powling
Dan Edwards
Daniel Baggott
Dave Christie-Miller
David Malakoty
David Roberts
Dawn Lindsay
Dean Phillips
Deborah Tayler
Derek Ward
Diney Crabtree
Dom Dol
Ed Whelpton
Elin Hopley
Eloise King-Smith
Emily Lauterpacht
Emily Leeming
Emma Priest
Emma Troughton
Faith Peace
Fiona Watson
Florence Haddock
Fred Leeming
George Emery
Georgia Buchanan
Georgie Futong
Georgina Valentine
Harry Leeming
Harry Whelpton
Helen Cook
Hermione Brown
Hester Rowell
India Volkers Poile
Isabel Crispin
James Robinson
Jane Stedman

Jane Whitelaw
Jo Caswell
Jo Duffield
Jo Ellis
Jo Parsons
Jody McCrystal
Joseph De Klee
Josephine King
Karen Mawson
Karen Richard
Kim Giddings
Laura Lockwood
Laura Verrechia
Lindsay Cooper
Lisa Mortimer
Lizzie Christie-Miller
Louisa Wentworth-Stanley
Louise Higgs
Lucy Sandys-Clarke
Lucy Watson
Matthew Brittle
Natali Shatchan
Neil Owens
Nick Rowan
Nicki Bell
Olivia Howard
Patricia Farrelly
Patricia Kirchner
Pip Clery
Pip Hall
Polly Bennett
Rachel Brown
Rachel De Wachter
Rebecca Blackfield
Rebecca Blackstone
Rebecca Harrington
Rebecca Ward
Rosemary Roberts
Rosie Atkinson
Sarah Whitehead
Sheila Gilmour
Sian Butler
Sophie Hammond
Sophie Whelpton
Stephanie Pettigrew
Stephanie Weiss
Stephen Blades
Stephen Christie-Miller
Susie Liddell
Susie Sampson
Suzanne Tuzes
Tara Pinches
Ted Christie-Miller
Terence Cunnane
Tobey Duncan
Victoria Crawford
Yumna Laher

Stephanie Brown

Dawn Lindsay

James Robinson

Jody McCrystal

Georgina Valentine

Rebecca and Derek Ward

INDEX

GLOSSARY

INGREDIENTS

Aubergine – eggplant
Beetroot – beets
Caster sugar – superfine sugar
Chicory – endive
Coriander (fresh) – cilantro
Courgette – zucchini
Double cream – heavy cream
Mangetout – snow peas
Natural yogurt – plain yogurt

Peppers (red/green/yellow) – bell peppers
Plain flour – all-purpose flour
Rapeseed oil – canola oil
Soured cream – sour cream
Spring onions – scallions
Stock – broth
Sultanas – golden raisins
Long-stem broccoli – broccolini
Tomato purée – tomato paste

EQUIPMENT

Baking paper – parchment paper
Griddle pan – grill pan
Grill – broiler
Roasting tray – roasting pan
Sieve – fine mesh strainer